DVIJA: A PROPHET UNHEARD

dvija

A PROPHET UNHEARD

T K MAHADEVAN

EWP

AFFILIATED **EAST-WEST PRESS PVT. LTD.**

NEW DELHI · MADRAS

Readers are warned not to quote Gandhi's words from this book, as these have been put through a transmutation process which, while leaving the substance intact, has taken creative liberties with the language.

© 1977 T. K. MAHADEVAN

Printed in India at Amra Press, 132 Lattice Bridge Road, Madras 600 041. Published by Affiliated East-West Press Private Limited 4C, Montieth Court, Madras 600 008.

To MOHANDAS KARAMCHAND GANDHI—
crank, prophet, genius, human . . .

मृत्युर्यस्योपसेचनम् ।

TO THE READER

WHEN the Publishers asked me to write for them a book on Gandhi, my first response was a violent shaking of the head. No no no! For god's sake, not *another* book on Gandhi! But they persisted and I brooded. After some months they won the day. So in a sense this is a loser's book—take it or leave it!

Why was I reluctant? For two reasons. First, Gandhi is his own best interpreter. His thinking is so lucid and he has the ability to put across his thoughts with such simple clarity that he doesn't need an outside interpreter. Secondly, the scores of books that have been, and continue to be, published on Gandhi, miss the core of the man by yards. It would be no exaggeration to say that Gandhi is the most misunderstood man of the twentieth century.

When, therefore, I agreed to write the book, my sole intention was to instil in you, not simply a curiosity about Gandhi, but a burning desire to read him in the original. Read Gandhi! Plough through sixty large volumes! (That's the figure at this writing: by the time the project is completed, Gandhi's collected works may approach ninety volumes!) Why, I must be mad!

Patience, dear reader. All I want you to do is to read just one of Gandhi's little books—*Hind Swaraj*. A mere 30,000 words: three hours of brisk reading, nothing more. But I want you to read it, as Gandhi kept vainly pleading, "with my eyes". Get under his skin. Feel things the way he felt them.

Not an easy task, I agree. But it has got to be done. Read *Hind Swaraj* if you love the human family and this earth which is our home. Read it if you wish to do your little bit to halt man's mad race towards self-extinction.

I have expatiated on the structure and style of my book, on what the exercise is all about, within the text itself. All I need to say here is that, in an extended sense, it is a study of the human condition from the point of view of Gandhi, and a study of Gandhi from the point of view of the human condition.

T. K. MAHADEVAN.

*The book is constructed
in three movements . . .*

STIGMATA

STIGMATA

Name: MOHANDAS KARAMCHAND GANDHI.

Sex: Male.

Age: Seventy-eight.

Cause of death: Accidental, having found himself in the path of two bullets, one directed at his chest, the other at his abdomen.

Name of assailant: It is not important.

Place of death: A garden, while going to a prayer meeting.

What happened immediately after death: Stupefaction. People ran about in terror.

Where was the deceased: He lay cradled in the lap of one of his followers, and was later carried into the house, bathed, and prepared for cremation.

Please describe the condition of the deceased: The flesh was firm and smooth. The body of a much younger man. No teeth, no hair, jug ears. Except for the marks left by the bullets and except for the fact that he was no longer breathing, he seemed to be alive.

Was this a miracle? No.

Date of death: January 30, 1948.

Date of birth: October 2, 1869.

Thus the autopsy of Gandhi in the poetic evocation of Robert Payne. I have borrowed it from his recently published *In a Nest of Flames*, a poem full of a strange tenderness and nostalgia.

But Gandhi died not in 1948. He died a good forty years earlier, in 1908. The last forty years of his life was a rebirth. In almost a literal sense, Gandhi was a *dvija*, a twice-born. You have to understand him as a *dvija* if you will understand him at all.

Gandhi's life falls into two neat halves, each of roughly forty years duration. The Gandhi that is widely known and written upon is the Gandhi of the second half. This may be said to be the popular Gandhi—the astute political strategist who fought the British empire with bare hands and won freedom for India. The story has been so often told that it will not bear repetition. Nor is such an exercise worthwhile, for it touches but the fringe of the man. My interest rather is in the Gandhi of the first half. Here was a relative non-celebrity, fighting not with an outside enemy but with the depths of his own soul, fighting not for his country, not even for his countrymen beleaguered in a foreign land, but for the larger human family, for the survival of the human race.

This Gandhi is little known and much less understood. Not even those who were closest to him in those dark days had the faintest idea what it was he was trying to communicate. Natural enough. They were men of small minds. Their horizons lay not farther than the reach of their limited visions. They were pettifoggers, self-centred creatures, entangled in the endless round of 'my family, my community, my country, my selfrespect.' In a word, the life of Gandhi—and here I mean both halves of it—

can be aptly described as the story of a giant trying hard, and tragically failing, to communicate with pigmies.

But prolonged failure of communication can be fatal in two ways. One way, whereby a prophet remains unheard, is well known. This kind of fatality is relatively harmless. It is the stuff of human history. Had prophets been heard—and heeded—history would have taken a different course. But the other way, whereby the prophet himself loses track of his prophecy, gives up his long vision and takes to the short cut, is tragic. It turns the course of history backwards. I have a fear that for much the larger part of what I have called his second birth, Gandhi allowed the block in communication to divert him from his major task. This diversion may have been, to him, nothing more than an exigent and marginal superficiality. To the others, the diversion provided a much needed alibi, allowing them to tailor Gandhi to their size and shape. So that from being an emancipator of man, Gandhi became—and remains—a mere liberator of the Indian nation. Destined to remain *sui generis*, a mind apart, Gandhi's interpreters turned him into a member of the common herd.

I began by making the startling assertion that Gandhi died not in 1948 but forty years earlier. Any alert reader would know that my reference is to the Pathan Mir Alam's almost fatal assault on Gandhi that took place in South Africa on the tenth of February 1908. If I were factually minded, I would certainly have used the phrase: 'almost died'. But what I am writing is an exercise in philosophical biography. While basing myself on incontrovertible evidence, I am trying to escape the shackles of mere factuality. Perhaps I am being presumptuous, but I have a notion that an excessive regard for facts distorts the sense of history and is wholly ruinous to biographical perception. A man's life is not what happens to him, nor what he does, from the cradle to the grave. It is not a meticulous—and often tiresomely lengthy—account of all the names, dates and events that figure in his life and how they are related to one another. Nor even of such of them as are significant. There are not several equally significant events in a man's life. Those who detect such a plurality and go to great lengths trying to fuse them into a unity (which generally crumbles at the merest touch) are merely being lazy. In every life there is only one event (or one person or place) that is truly significant. A commanding height, a turning point, a watershed. The function of philosophical biography is to locate this: the rest follows as a matter of course. But this process of locating the turning point is a very painstaking one. You have to do it to a nicety or the whole exercise falls to the ground.

I have said that Gandhi's life falls into two neat halves and that I intend concentrating on the first half. The reader should not assume from this that I shall be retelling the oft-told story of Gandhi's ancestry, parentage, birth and upbringing, his youthful misadventures, his search for a place in society and so on—and then suddenly leave the story hanging in midair. That would be a case of the cure being worse than the cold. In fact, a good part of the first forty years—barring certain adventitious and over-narrated happenings—bears hardly any foot-

prints that could be truly called significant. Nothing here
to fix your grip on. No signs of greatness. And yet, an inner voice (shall we say) tells me that the second half of
Gandhi's life would be inexplicable without that something that happened to him within the first half. A prophet does not issue out of a vacuum.   A prophet is made.

Now when, where and how did that concatenation of
circumstances take place which, taken in the round, could
be said to have, as it were, catapulted the pleader into the
realm of prophecy? I think it all happened when Gandhi
was nearing the age of forty—a dangerous age for most
people anyway. My essay will therefore concentrate on a
very brief period— let us say, between 1908 and 1910—
and try to discover there the makings of the prophet who,
alas, remained for the rest of his life, and largely even now,
unperceived, unheard and unheeded. It is a tragedy
too sad for words and one that can be explained, if at
all, only by means of a philosophical subterfuge—
namely, our continuing failure to recognize the *dvija*, the
twice-born, in Gandhi. To put it in the simplest terms,
when a man dies and is reborn—he is a new man. Am I
indulging in a metaphor, a philosophical conceit, or is
there a fair enough approximation to the truth in this,
somewhat arrogant, asseveration? We shall see as we
proceed.

Here is how Gandhi narrates the circumstances of his
first death. A bright February morning in Johannesburg.
'When at a quarter to ten I set out towards the Registration Office, in the company of Mr. Essop Mia, Mr. Naidoo
and a few other Indians, I did feel that there might be an

attack on me. In fact, I had spotted two of the assailants near the office. They walked alongside of us. I then became surer. But I decided that I should not mind being assaulted by my own brethren.

'Some way ahead, one of the men asked, "Where are you all going?" Mr. Essop Mia was about to answer, when I interrupted, saying, "I am going to give my finger-impressions. The others too will do the same. If you want to give your thumb-impressions only, you may do so".'

The world has changed a lot since the beginning of the century that a reader living in the mid-seventies, to whom this book is primarily addressed, will find all this rigma-role about finger-impressions and thumb-impressions a little too difficult to understand. Hence let me interrupt Gandhi's vivid narrative for a brief excursion into the bizarre history of those times.

This business of compelling persons, who are not other-wise criminals, to give impressions of their ten fingers or their two thumbs had to do with the Immigration Act of the Transvaal. Ever willing as he was to make a short-term compromise in order to gain a long-term advantage —which, of course, is the essence of good politics— Gandhi had no difficulty in understanding the crux of the situation. But he found it no easy task taking all his fellow countrymen along with him. The communica-tion block! The leit-motif of Gandhi's entire life!

Here is a typical example: 'I feel ashamed for the community that I should still have to write about finger-impressions. The point is so simple that it is difficult to understand why it is still being argued. But the late Professor Max Muller said that as long as the truth is not

18

effectively impressed on the mind of the other, there is nothing wrong in repeating the same thing over and over again in different words.'

What a monument of patience and perseverance!

Under the Immigration Act, the compulsion to give finger-impressions (with certain marginal variations) applied to all immigrants, such as working-class whites, and not only to those of Indian origin.

Argued Gandhi: 'How can the Indian community protest against these regulations when the whites do not? The reason is worth noting. The whites are free and independent. They do not get scared unnecessarily, neither do they see humiliation where there is none. They do not feel that finger-impressions by themselves imply criminality, although it is true that this method was at first applied only to criminals. The fact is that for identification of pass-holders and for prevention of fraud, digit-impressions offer a simple, effective and scientific means.'

Watch the persuasiveness of Gandhi's logic: 'When Mr. Jenner discovered vaccination with cow-pox serum, he first tried it on prisoners. It was introduced among the rest of the population after the experiment had proved successful. No one could argue that the free population was thereby humiliated!

'If any one wants to know why all these arguments were not advanced earlier, it is easy to answer the question. Formerly, finger-prints were a part of an enslaving law and therefore a symbol of our slavery. It was thus our duty to draw attention to the humiliation of giving finger-impressions.

'If anywhere in the world they should enforce finger-impressions or even a thumb-impression on the Indian community alone, with the object of stigmatizing it for the colour of its skin, we will take up the banner once again.

'Besides, everyone must know that our campaign in the past was not directed against finger-impressions as such but against the law. The repeal of the law being now assured, the Indian sword returns, on its own as it were, to the scabbard.'

Alas, to no avail had Gandhi argued with his countrymen. For some of them, like Mir Alam, saw in his new stance a betrayal of the Indian cause.

To return to Gandhi's narrative: 'My only recollection of what followed is that I received very severe blows on my left ribs. I do not remember the manner of the assault, but people say that I fell down unconscious with the first blow, which was delivered with a stick. Then my assailants struck me with an iron pipe, and they also kicked me. Thinking me dead, they stopped.

'I have an impression that as the blows started I uttered the words, "He Rama!" Later, as I came to, I got up with a smile. In my mind there was not the slightest anger or hatred for the assailants.

'I was taken to Mr. Gibson's office, opposite which I had been attacked. A doctor washed the wounds and they were thinking of removing me to hospital. Mr. Doke, a clergyman, hurried to the spot on hearing news of the assault. He suggested that I should be taken to his place. After some deliberation I agreed.

'Mr. Doke is not exactly a friend. I had met him barely three or four times before then, and that to explain the nature of the Indian campaign to him. It was thus a stranger that he took into his house. All the members of his family remained in constant attendance on me.

'Both the blows and the injuries I received were severe, but in the opinion of the doctor not many patients were known to recover as speedily as I did. Apart from the wounds, my mouth was swollen and so was my forehead. A poultice of clean earth was put on these, and the swelling has now subsided. I had been badly hit in the ribs, and here again the recovery is nearly complete, thanks to a large poultice of earth.'

In the course of the narrative, Gandhi reflected on death. 'I feel that we fear death needlessly. I have not known such fear for a long time now, and I have grown more fearless after this incident.'

Gandhi's account of his close brush with death is particularly memorable for the note of compassion, forgiveness and self-suffering that runs through it: 'I do not blame anyone for the assault. Those who attacked me did so in the belief that I had done the community harm.

'Some people know of only one way of expressing disapproval. For them physical strength is the supreme thing. How then could I be angry? What point would there be in having them prosecuted? My real duty consists in disproving their charge against me. That will take time. Meanwhile, as is the way of the world, people will persist in the methods of violence. The duty of the wise man is but to bear the suffering in patience. I have therefore no choice but to endure the suffering inflicted on me.'

Years later, now in India, Gandhi recollected the Mir Alam assault and ruminated over the nature of violence and nonviolence. 'Violence,' he said, 'is a power in the world today and we are apt to be unnerved in the face of it. If, however, we calmly think about it we shall find that there is no reason for nervousness.

'Just suppose that Mir Alam and his friends, instead of only wounding, had actually destroyed my body. And suppose also that the community had deliberately remained calm and unperturbed, and forgiven the offenders perceiving that according to their lights they could not behave otherwise than they did. Far from injuring the community, such a noble attitude would have greatly benefited them. All misunderstanding would have disappeared, and Mir Alam and party would have had their eyes opened to the error of their ways. As for me, nothing better can happen to a satyagrahi than meeting death all unsought in the very act of satyagraha, that is, pursuing truth.'

It is a noble statement, but how much of it may seen incoherent or incomprehensible to a mind not in tune with Gandhi's innovative ways of thinking. That block in communication again!

Alert as usual, Gandhi clarifies his propositions. They are true, he says, 'only of a struggle like the satyagraha movement, where there is no room for hatred, where self-reliance is the order of the day, where no one has to look expectantly at another, where there are no leaders and hence no followers—or where all are leaders and all are followers—so that the death of a fighter, however eminent, makes not for slackness but on the other hand intensifies the struggle.'

Meanwhile General Smuts had committed his famous 'breach of faith.' The phrase is Gandhi's and he admitted to being ashamed of using it, since it reflected 'the obliquity of human nature.' Perhaps all that happened between Smuts and Gandhi was simply a block in communication—but a block of a more complex nature. For 'Slim Janny' (as Jan Smuts was facetiously referred to by his fellow South Africans) was 'a very clever man and a trimmer whose words were intelligible only to himself, and often such that either party could interpret them in a sense favourable to himself.' The description, harshly sarcastic though it is, is also Gandhi's.

He goes on: 'Indeed, on a suitable occasion he would lay aside the interpretations of both the parties, put a fresh interpretation upon them, carry it out and support it by such clever arguments that the parties, for the time, would be led to imagine that they were wrong and Smuts was right!'

Perhaps one could describe these infructuous goings-on between Smuts and Gandhi as a confrontation between the clever quibble and the naivete of truth. But Gandhi's truth was never easily worsted. Nevertheless, for a leader to have to change his stance within such frequent intervals and thus almost to lose his credibility with his people (all because of an inborn trust in the goodness of man) is the kind of humiliation which even a Gandhi cannot swallow.

Take a look at the evidence. First we see Gandhi rousing his fellow-Indians against giving their finger-impressions, on the ground that 'in India finger-prints were taken only of criminals.' Then, taken in by Slim Janny's equivocation, we find him defending the system of finger-impressions and persuading his followers to apply for and take out certificates of registration bearing the tell-tale smudges. Finally, back to square one, we find him once again in the garb of the rabble rouser.

The scene: the Fordsburg mosque in Johannesburg. The time: a Sunday afternoon in August 1908, half a year after the Mir Alam killing. A crowd of three thousand Indian men and women milling around, within and beyond the courtyard of the mosque, waiting for the dramatic moment.

Gandhi rises to address the gathering. 'I have been taken to task, I have been ridiculed,' he begins. 'And yet, the advice that I have ventured to give to my fellow-countrymen, I am going to repeat this afternoon: We must burn our certificates!'

As the thunderous applause dies down, he goes on in measured tones: 'I am told that I may be instrumental in imposing on my countrymen untold suffering because of the advice that I have given. I know that well. But I do know this also: that the keeping of these certificates will impose on my countrymen untold indignity. And I say this with the greatest emphasis at my command, that I would far rather that my countrymen suffered all they have to suffer than submit to indignity.

'I did not come out of jail before my time was up merely to leave the hardships I was suffering there. Personally, I was not undergoing any hardships whatever. It would be a far greater hardship to me to have to submit to indignity, or to see a fellow-countryman trampled underfoot or his bread taken away from him.

'No, gentlemen, the servant who stands before you this afternoon is not made of that stuff. It is because I ask you to suffer everything than break your oath, it is because I expect my countrymen to be true to their God—that I ask you this afternoon to burn all these certificates.'

Cries of 'We are ready to burn them!' rend the air. A large three-legged pot is then filled with the registration certificates, paraffin poured in and the whole thing set on fire, amidst scenes of the wildest enthusiasm. The crowd hurrahs and shouts itself hoarse. Hats are thrown in the air, and whistles blown. . .

The Pathans had not only tried to finish off Gandhi, but they also belaboured Essop Mia, chairman of the British Indian Association, a few months later, for having given evidence against them in what I shall, within the meaning of my essay, call the first Gandhi 'murder' case.

Gandhi's reaction to this repeated act of cowardice is worth recalling: 'If the Pathans believe that they can terrorize the poor Indians, they are mistaken. In the near future, if not today, the Indian community will learn to be courageous and defend itself.

'It is possible to defend oneself in two ways. The better way is not to defend oneself at all and to accept blows with courage. We see everywhere that force which does not meet with any resistance at all is wasted. If we punch at the air, the arm will only feel a wrench. If someone swears at me and I do not swear back, he will soon become silent, having exhausted himself. The same is true of a man who uses violence to attack another.

'Till one acquires this kind of courage, it is necessary to cultivate the strength to defend oneself. It is not difficult to defend oneself with a stick, or in some other

suitable fashion. The important thing is to be fearless.
If one receives a blow, one must have the strength to
strike back in self-defence.

'My considered view is that, if we can develop real
courage, we should suffer assault rather than turn away
from our duty out of fear of violence. If, however, such
courage is beyond our reach, we must learn to keep the
stick with us and be prepared to defend ourselves with it.
This is also part of satyagraha. A satyagrahi will adhere
to truth to the last.'

Notice here the slow and cautious development of
Gandhi's core idea of satyagraha. We shall watch this
development, step by step, as we go along. What I am
attempting in this essay is to pick up beads of various
sizes, shapes and colours, from this (as it seems to me)
central period of his life, and to string them haphazardly
upon the Gandhian thread of truth, in the belief that
what will result will be a garland worth wearing.

A bead larger than life, from this period, is what has
been called *A Dialogue on the Compromise*. A fascinating
document, both on account of its style and content, this
rather long essay was doubtless written before the Mir
Alam assault, but published in his weekly paper, *Indian
Opinion*, some days thereafter. The dialogic style foreshadows *Hind Swaraj*, the great short book he wrote some
twenty traumatic months later and to which I shall revert
from time to time.

However, unlike as in *Hind Swaraj*, here the Editor
begins by hoisting a warning signal. What Gandhi says
in this short prefatory paragraph is so pertinent to the

question of communication—or rather, to the non-communication syndrome which has, from the very start, bedevilled our understanding of the peculiar cast of his mind—that I must quote from it.

'I should like,' says the Editor to the Reader, 'to remind you of one thing before you ask any questions. An answer, they say, has no meaning except for one who is equipped to understand it. For instance, if anyone asks a question about multiplication and division while knowing nothing of addition and subtraction, he is not equipped to understand the answer. In the same way, you should have the following qualification for asking questions: you should ask them in the presence of God, with sincere and patriotic intention. If you do, you will have no difficulty in following the answers.'

In *Hind Swaraj*, on the other hand, the Editor begins by stressing his own functional responsibility rather than that of the Reader. Says he: 'One of the objects of a newspaper [in this case, *Indian Opinion*] is to understand popular feeling and to give expression to it. Another is to arouse among the people certain desirable sentiments. And the third is fearlessly to expose popular defects, whatever the difficulties in the ways. The exercise of all these three functions is involved in answering your question.'

Be that as it may. After cautioning the reader, Gandhi proceeds, in the Dialogue, to come to terms with some very thorny questions. One of these concerns, of course, the finger-impressions. Not entirely convinced with Gandhi's circumlocutory answers to his question touching compulsory and voluntary registration, the Reader hazards the view that the whole subterfuge appears to him to be designed to protect the interests of the rich and the educated at the expense of the vast mass of poor and illiterate immigrants.

Gandhi takes the insinuation in his stride, but he parries it somewhat unconvincingly. After all, argues Gandhi, 'educated persons and men of means and standing can be identified by the knowledge they possess and by their appearance. It is humiliating to them even to be asked to give finger-impressions. Looking at it thus, it does not appear wrong that illiterate persons who are not otherwise known should have to give their finger-impressions. Men of standing can leave Durban without taking out a certificate, but an illiterate person or one not otherwise known would come to grief by following their example. He would find it difficult to return.'

By their appearance? This is strange logic. Do all poor people—like crows, say—look alike? This is insulting. If one rich man can be distinguished from another rich man by his appearance—whatever that phrase may mean—why not one poor man from another poor man? Again, if it is humiliating to a rich man to give his finger-impressions, why should it be otherwise in the case of the poor? One can only assume that here Gandhi was nodding or that he was writing in a hurry. Fortunately, such forced, careless (or even callous) thinking is rare in him.

On the other hand, it is not impossible that when Gandhi wrote the *Dialogue* he was under great mental distress. For wasn't he pleading for the very same thing he had been battling against for so many months? You first decry finger-impressions as a stigma; then you decoy your people to wear that very same stigma! Although

Gandhi had his arguments pat, not many were convinced. After all, a stigma does not turn overnight into an ornament. And Gandhi, with his antennae alert as ever, sensed the tension and anger his sudden turnabout was causing among his people. But the death-wish in him was asserting itself and there was no holding him back. You may, if you like, call it his truth-fixation.

On the surface, this kind of one-track thinking may seem a weakness. Indeed, it is so in the case of most people. But in Gandhi it was the very secret of his towering greatness. Vincent Sheean, I believe, was the first to detect this pathological trait in him. 'There was something stricken about Gandhi,' Sheean lamented. 'He behaved like a specific instrument of a specific purpose, from the beginning to the end of his life.'

Sheean's observation, of course, related to Gandhi's strange lack of interest, not to say involvement, in the struggle of the African peoples themselves. This point, however, has been made in a few other studies as well, and it is no part of my purpose to tread on beaten ground. Nevertheless, it seems relevant that I should, within the narrow ambit of my essay, attempt a clarification of what has been unjustly described as a mystery.

Gandhi was not in South Africa to fight every battle that came his way. He was there to steel himself, school himself, put his ideas and ideals into a coherent system— for the great single battle that, as he somewhat ambitiously thought, lay ahead of him. Where? Of course, back in India. But it was not to be a battle for India so much as for the larger human family. India was simply the most suitable ground—the dharmakshetra—for that battle. If he wore blinkers, he did so deliberately, in order that he may not fritter away his limited resources of time and energy or be diverted from his chosen goal. But of this later.

Meanwhile the white man's press in South Africa, taking advantage of Gandhi's readiness to compromise on the ten-finger business, was carrying on a campaign of taunt and slander against the Indian community. *The Transvaal Critic*, for example, published an obnoxiously humorous cartoon, depicting Gandhi 'seated on a chair in great dignity and signing his name, while other Indians, miserable creatures, keep standing as they give their finger-impressions, with large drops of black ink dripping from their fingers'. Look, the paper seemed to say: one law for Gandhi the advocate, another law for Ganapati the street-hawker!

When the Reader (in the *Dialogue*) pointed this out angrily—and especially to the fact that *Indian Opinion*, which had once fought against class distinctions was now covertly supporting them—Gandhi again prevaricated. He argued, with a speciousness which ill befits a satyagrahi, that 'there is a great deal of difference between our asking for special privileges and the government offering them on its own. It would have been improper to reject what the government offered us as a right.' Is that so? The later Gandhi would have instantly noticed the hollowness of this kind of defence.

Incredibly he went on: 'There are natural distinctions of class which no one can oppose. Our fight is against artificial class distinctions. The important thing is that well-placed persons [i.e. those who do not have to disfigure their ten fingers with black ink] should regard themselves as trustees of the poor.'

How nice! If I have dwelt at too great a length on this unreal and antiquarian question of the finger-impressions—unreal and antiquarian to us of the present day that is—I did so because it brings out with great clarity the nucleal shape of some of Gandhi's core ideas.

And—lest we forget—it also led to Gandhi's first death. After that close shave, he was no longer the same man who wrote the *Dialogue*. Mir Alam was the instrument of this transmutation. Hence-forward, as I shall try to show, Gandhi's journey will take him directly to the writing of his great manifesto, *Hind Swaraj*.

TRAUMATA

TRAUMATA

At this point, I should like to give the reader a fore-taste of the unusual structure of this unusual book on Gandhi. In my mind, the book falls into three parts: let me call them (a) Stigmata, (b) Traumata, and (c) Chiliasm. I have chosen terms with a faintly theological ring about them in order to emphasize the philosophical nature of my essay. The expressionistic style in which, for the most part, it is being written is also deliberate. Perhaps the reader may find it unnecessarily idosyn-cratic at places. At others he may notice a light-hearted-ness which, conditioned as he is to the extant heavy literature on Gandhi, he would find jarring. But I would ask him to bear with these quirks. This is not *another* book on Gandhi, but rather a *new kind* of book on a much-written subject. In trying my hand at it, the intention is not so much to achieve some sort of novelty as to shock the reader out of certain set patterns and ideas that have, for over a quarter of a century, been handed down to him as constituting the essence of Gandhi. In other words, this book may be said to be an exercise in deconditioning.

A prophet, I have asserted earlier on, does not issue out of a vacuum; he is made. He is hammered out on the anvil of unexpected happenings. He has almost to walk over a bed of red-hot coals. In fact, as I have emphasized — and as I shall continue to emphasize

—he has to die and be reborn. He has to be a *dvija*.

In the first brief part, 'Stigmata', which we have just completed, we saw Gandhi pass through some of these essential stages. He fought against the stigmatization of a whole people—seesawing from one position to another and, in the process, achieving his death-wish. He invited upon himself, willingly, the stigma attaching to his poorer brethren. He displayed his political acumen in the artlessly artful manner in which he manipulated both his people and the government. (This conscious procrusteanism of Gandhi so characteristic of him comes out succinctly well in something he said years later in another context: 'Mine is but to fight for my meaning, no matter whether I win or lose!')

Being necessarily a short essay, I could not do much more than pick out for the reader random glimpses. If he has the patience, I would refer him to the voluminous pages of Gandhi's *Collected Works*. But he is warned. Unless he has his bearings right, he will come out a confused man.

Now for the 'Traumata'.

The tenth of January 1908, a clear month before the Mir Alam assault. Sunny morning, within the precincts of the Newtown mosque in Johannesburg. Gandhi had been summoned to attend court to receive sentence for disobeying eviction orders, but for some reason the hearing was put off to the afternoon. Alert as ever, Gandhi decided to make good use of the few intervening hours to address a hurriedly arranged meeting of his countrymen—a sort of valedictory exhortation to the

36

rank and file to stand firm while he and other leaders would be in prison.

The large and excited crowd that had gathered outside the court now troop into the precincts of the mosque. A makeshift platform is set up quickly and seating arrangements for the audience are made with the help of thousands of serviceable paraffin tins found lying around the place.

Gandhi rises to speak, first in Hindustani, then in English. 'All of us who are to go to jail today are not at all afraid. On the contrary, we look upon it as an opportunity to serve our country and to show the government that we are men, not dogs.

'I stand here today to give you all my last word. It may be only for a month, or for two months, or even for six months. And my last word is: do not deceive yourselves, do not deceive the government, do not deceive your humble servant.

'For the thousandth time I wish to repeat that the law we are disobeying is not simply a question of giving one thumb-impression or ten digit-impressions. It is its underlying spirit that we are shunning, for it condemns the whole of the Indian community.

'When I last went to England as your servant, a gentleman on board the ship said, "I see you are going to London to get rid of the dog's collar." Precisely. It is because we do not want to wear a dog's collar that we have put up this fight.

'No matter what others may say, this is a struggle for religious liberty. By religion, I do not mean formal or customary religion, but that which underlies all religions and brings us face to face with our Maker. If on taking a deliberate vow we break it in order to remain in the Transvaal without physical inconvenience, we cease to be men and we forsake our God.

'Jesus had said that those who would follow God must leave the world. In that same spirit I ask you all to leave the world and cling to God, as a child clings to his mother's breast. Then I have not the slightest doubt that this struggle can have but one issue.'

Two o'clock in the afternoon of the same day. The eastern side of Government Square, Johannesburg. A continuous stream of excited Indians pouring into the square. It had begun to drizzle. Enter Gandhi, reading the first edition of *The Star*, while his admirers walk alongside, sheltering him with umbrellas.

Inside the court, at a quarter past two.

Magistrate: 'Have you any questions to ask?'

Gandhi: 'No, sir'.

On the prosecution proceedings being concluded, Gandhi obtained leave to make a short statement.

'Sir', he said, 'I think a distinction ought to be made between my case and those which are to follow. I have just received a message from Pretoria that my compatriots there had been tried and sentenced to three months' hard labour. If these men had committed an offence, I have committed a greater one, and I ask you to impose on me the heaviest penalty.'

Magistrate: 'You asked for the heaviest penalty which the law authorizes?'

Gandhi: 'Yes, sir'.

Magistrate: 'I must say I do not feel inclined to accede to your request. Six months' hard labour, with a fine of 500 pounds, appears to me to be totally out of proportion to the offence you have committed. I think a fair sentence would be two months' imprisonment without hard labour.'

Years later Gandhi recalled the scene with a touch of unusual sentimentality: 'On the sentence being pronounced, I was at once removed in custody and was then quite alone. The policeman asked me to sit on a bench kept there for prisoners, shut the door on me and went away. I was somewhat agitated and fell into deep thought. Home, the courts where I practised, the public meeting—all these passed away like a dream, and I was now a prisoner.

'What will happen in two months? Will I have to serve the full term? If the people courted imprisonment in large numbers, as they had promised, there would be no question of serving the full sentence. But if they failed to fill the prisons, two months would be as tedious as an age.

'These thoughts passed through my mind and they filled me with shame. How vain I was! I who had asked the people to consider the prisons as His Majesty's hotels; the suffering consequent upon disobeying the Black Act as perfect bliss; and the sacrifice of one's all and of life itself, in resisting it, as supreme enjoyment! Where had all this knowledge vanished today? This second train of

thought acted upon me as a bracing tonic and I began to
laugh at my own folly.'

Towards evening of the same day. In a Johannesburg
prison-yard. Gandhi's fellow-convicts were three Indians
and two Chinese. 'First, all of us were weighed,' reports
Gandhi. 'Then we were asked to give our finger-impressions. After being stripped we were given prison uniforms
to wear, consisting of black trousers, a shirt, a jumper, a
cap and socks. We were given a bag each to pack away
our own clothes in. Before being led off to our ward, we
were each given eight ounces of bread. We were then
marched off to a prison intended for Kaffirs.

'There our garments were stamped with the letter N—
which meant that we were being classed with the Natives.
We were all prepared for hardships, but not quite for
this experience. We could understand not being classed
with the whites, but to be placed on the same level with
the Natives seemed too much to put up with. I then felt
that Indians had not launched on passive resistance too
soon. Here was further proof that the obnoxious law was
intended to emasculate the Indians.

'The cells for Kaffirs were adjacent to ours. They used
to make a frightful din in their cells as also in the adjoin-
ing yard. We were given a separate ward because we
were sentenced to simple imprisonment. Otherwise we
would have been in the same ward with them.

'Apart from whether or not this implies degradation,
I must say it is rather dangerous. Kaffirs are as a rule
uncivilized—the convicts even more so. They are
troublesome, very dirty and live almost like animals.

They often started rows and fought among themselves. 'Besides us, there were hardly three or four Indian prisoners in the whole jail. They were locked up with the Kaffirs. Imagine the plight of these poor Indians thrown into such company!'

The streak of racial superiority—well, it can't be anything else—which runs through this account may be another reason that Gandhi could not identify himself with the land of his temporary adoption or with the struggles of its own peoples. At any rate, one heaves a sigh of relief, as one overhears the torment in Gandhi's mind, that the magistrate refused to accede to his obsessional request for six month's hard labour, which would certainly have thrown him among the Kaffir 'animals'.

Within ten days, with more Indian passive resisters pouring into jail, Gandhi had on his hands a major problem—that of securing for them a diet to which they are habituated. This was not easy, for the jail regulations had not taken into account Indian dietary inhibitions and susceptibilities. Nor could they have done so, since these latter are a world in themselves.

However, Gandhi was never at his best as when he was face to face with a problem—the more intractable the better! He dashed off a petition, on behalf of his suffering fellow-prisoners, to the Director of Prisons. It is characteristic of Gandhi that it is the suffering of others, rather than his own, that sparked off the complaints. For he himself had been partaking of this same food—unfamiliar and constitutionally injurious though it was—without so much as breathing a word.

What was the food like? 'For the first week', reports Gandhi, 'we were served with twelve ounces of mealie pap. Most of us had more of the spoon than of the porridge for the first breakfast.' The porridge, of course, contained neither milk nor sugar. Dinner consisted of twelve ounces of beans. And for supper they had four ounces of rice with an ounce of ghee.

'For most of us, it meant practically starvation. Even when we got over the natural repugnance, it was a diet that constipated some of us and gave others diarrhoea. But we were determined to go through it and not ask for favours or concessions.

'In the second week the scale was a little relieved by the addition of eight ounces of vegetables, and on Sundays twelve ounces of meat. (Gandhi, of course, had another eight ounces of vegetables instead of the meat!) However, this diet did not last long.

'Now let us glance at the scale for European prisoners. For breakfast: one pint of porridge and four ounces of bread. Dinner: eight ounces of bread, together with meat or vegetables. Supper: eight ounces of bread, one pint of porridge and a drink of cocoa.

'It may be possible to reconcile oneself to the Europeans getting a *variety* of foods. But why should they get more in quantity? Have they a greater appetite than the Indians?'

Concluding the report, Gandhi falls into a mood of lamentation and resignation: 'Whereas both Kaffirs and Europeans get food suited to their tastes, nobody bothers about the poor Indians. They cannot get the food they want. If they are given European food, the whites will feel insulted. There is therefore nothing for it but to let themselves be classed with the Kaffirs and starve!'

Then he gives up the plaintive tone and looks at the larger issue of courting voluntary imprisonment. 'If there were no hardships,' he argues, 'what would be the point of being imprisoned? Moreover, we should give up clinging so tenaciously to our customs and habits. Out of regard for the country in which we live, we must accept the food grown in the soil of that country. And since there may be many occasions yet for us to go to jail, we should all get used to mealie pap.'

Other highlights of Gandhi's first experience of jail life are worth recalling. I shall continue the narration in Gandhi's own words, following as hitherto (and through-out the book) the method of creative abstracting, where-by one achieves brevity without sacrifice of the sense and spirit of the original.

Talking of his prison cell, Gandhi writes: 'It was a novel sensation to be locked up at half-past five. The cell was a galvanized-iron construction, fairly strong, though none too strong for prisoners bent on escaping. There was perhaps fair ventilation, and I was assured that these cells were the best ventilated of all the prisons in the Transvaal.

'The cell had an electric lamp, but it was not bright enough in which to do any reading in comfort. The light was switched off at eight o'clock in the evening and was spasmodically switched on and off during the night.

'Our bedding consisted of wooden planks fixed to three-inch-high legs, two blankets, an apology for a pillow, and matting. At our request, the governor of the jail ordered a table and two benches to be placed in the room for writing purposes.'

One of the prison rules was that every prisoner sentenced to two or more months had to have his hair cropped close and his moustache shaved off. 'In this connection,' writes Gandhi, 'I had an amusing experience. Although I knew that the rule was not rigorously enforced in the case of Indians, I was determined to go through all the experiences of a prisoner. I therefore asked the chief warder to have my hair cropped and my moustache shaved off. He told me the governor had strictly forbidden that. To allay suspicions, I offered to state in writing that I wanted the cropping of my own free will and for my own convenience. At last, after much dilly-dallying, the clippers and scissors arrived, and I and my fellow-prisoner Naidoo, who was a master of the tonsorial art, set to work. Soon the others followed suit—and all of us looked the smarter for it!'

Alas, Gandhi's 'happy' days in prison did not last the full term of two months. For through the mediatory efforts of friends, the government and the Indian community were well on the way to a settlement. And on the thirtieth of January, within hardly three weeks, Gandhi's first incarceration came to an end when he was taken to Pretoria to meet Smuts. By then the Indian influx into the cramped Johannesburg jail had swelled to a little over 160 prisoners. His Majesty's Hotel had never had such roaring business before!

The *Transvaal Leader*, which first reported Gandhi's unexpected release, carried the following story: 'Yesterday morning some Indian hawkers saw, as they believed, Mr. Gandhi proceed to the railway station in the company of another gentleman, who proved to be Supdt. Vernon of the Fordsburg police station. There was however no certainty that it was Mr. Gandhi [close cropped and minus his moustache, as he must have been] and the fact of his having been seen was the basis of an interesting rumour only. As a fact, the hawkers were quite correct in their conjecture. For about a quarter past eleven in the morning, Mr. Gandhi left the Fort for Park Station, whence he proceeded with Supdt. Vernon to Pretoria.

'But Mr. Gandhi's release came as a great surprise to his compatriots last night. Mr. Gandhi returned from Pretoria at ten o'clock and there was no one to meet him except Mr. Essop Mia—so well had the secret been kept. A *Leader* representative sought an interview with Mr. Gandhi after his arrival. In general health he seemed none the worse for his recent experiences, and was quite cheerful.'

A *Rand Daily Mail* reporter also interviewed him on his release. 'Honourable to both sides, Mr. Gandhi?' asked the reporter, referring to the compromise settlement. 'Perfectly,' said Gandhi. 'Then it is no climb-down?' persisted the reporter. 'Absolutely not,' said Gandhi.

Noticing his new tonsorial appearance, the reporter asked Gandhi if he had been subjected to the regulations usually applied to criminals. 'Oh no, this is all my own doing, said Gandhi with a chuckle.'

What transpired at the meeting between him and Smuts in Pretoria? Something on these lines:

Smuts: Personally I have nothing against the Indian community. But your demands are excessive. Even so I'll accept them. However, a word of warning. Don't let your people discuss these matters in public. Then my people will turn against me and you will be the loser.

Gandhi: I understand. Now where do we stand on the question of finger-impressions?

Smuts: Why are you raking up that subject all over again? I thought you said your resistance is not against it at all.

Gandhi: Yes, but what's your present thinking on it?

Smuts: Well, I suppose you'll have to give them if Government finds it necessary. But don't get worked up. We'll talk about it later.

[*Gandhi fidgets in his seat.*]

Smuts: And one thing more: don't let your people go harassing the blacklegs.

Gandhi: Of course you don't have to tell us that. We know they are doing wrong, but they are our brethren. They are our flesh and blood. How can any decent Indian harbour vengeful thoughts against them?...

In more ways than one, this first sojourn in jail, the sudden release, the willingness to suffer oneself while fighting for the needs of his fellow-prisoners—all these were characteristic of the thorny road his life was to take in the years and months ahead. First in South Africa and then in India, jails were to be Gandhi's second home. Characteristic too was the speed with which he turned this second home into a sort of Home University. For it was here, in the jails, that he did most of his reading. Once outside them, his life was never his own. Too much bustle. Too many calls on his time. And, of course, too many irons in the fire.

Of course Gandhi hadn't expected his early release. So he set about planning a course of study for two months. He made a beeline to the jail library: 'I borrowed some of Carlyle's works and the Bible. From a Chinese interpreter who used to visit the place, I borrowed a copy of the Koran in English, Huxley's lectures, Carlyle's biographies of Burns, Johnson and Scott, and Bacon's essays on civil and moral counsel.

'I also had some books of my own. These included an edition of the *Gita*, with a commentary by Manilal Dwivedi, some Tamil books, an Urdu book presented by Maulvi Saheb, and the writings of Tolstoy, Ruskin and Socrates. Most of these books I either read or re-read during my stay in jail.

'I used to study Tamil regularly. In the morning I read the Gita and in the afternoon portions of the Koran. In the evening I used to explain the Bible to Mr. Fortoen, a Chinese Christian. As he wished to learn English, I taught it to him through the Bible.

'If I were to serve my full term, I had intended to complete the translation of one of Carlyle's books and another of Ruskin. These books would have kept me wholly occupied.

'During the last days, a few books of Gujarati songs arrived, and many of us read these. But I would not call this reading to some purpose.

'If I had been awarded a longer term of imprisonment, I wouldn't have found it irksome. Indeed I would have added usefully to my knowledge. I believe that anyone who enjoys reading good books can easily bear to be alone anywhere.'

Spending intermittent and long terms in jail became so closely integrated with his life-style, that one shudders to think what would have happened to him without them. Would he have grown into the colossus that he eventually became, or would he have remained merely a court pleader, a petitioner on behalf of lost causes, an obstreperous pamphleteer—and, of course, a more devoted parent? One thing, however, seems clear to me. Without these long spells in jail, he would have remained comparatively ill-read and his mind would scarcely have foliated outwardly in so many directions or inwardly into those strange depths of political insight which are still the wonder of every serious student of his thought.

With the satyagraha called off, the jails emptied and the compromise document safely in his hands, Smuts did exactly what almost everyone in the Indian community, with the sole exception of Gandhi, had expected him to do. He went back on his word. Instead of repealing the Black Act, he took one step forward and put it firmly on the statute book.

'I was simply astounded,' confessed Gandhi. 'I did

not know how I would face the community. Here was
excellent food for my Pathan opponents. But far from
shaking my faith in satyagraha, this blow only made my
faith in it stronger.'

At the committee meeting that followed this shock,
Gandhi was severely taunted by fellow members. 'There
you are!' they said. 'You are very credulous. You
believe anything that anyone may say. And it is the
community that has to suffer for your credulity.'

They went on: 'You know what stuff we Indians are
made of. Our momentary enthusiasm must be taken at
the flood. If you neglect the temporary tide, you are
done for. How, alas, can we now rouse our people to
action again?'

Gandhi listened in stony silence, but with a wry smile
on his face. He was used to such setbacks. 'Well,'
he said, 'what you call my credulity is part and parcel of
me. It is really not credulity but trust, and it is the duty
of every one of us to trust our fellowmen. Even granting
I am credulous, you must take me as you find me.

'In great struggles like ours, there is always a tide and
an ebb. However clear may be your understanding
with the adversary, what is there to prevent him from
breaking faith? Aren't there among us many who
readily pass promissory notes without any intention of
paying up when they fall due?

'There is only one remedy, and that lies in our hands.
Ignore the law and resume satyagraha. It is not as if the
sword of satyagraha can be used only once and becomes
useless afterwards. Satyagraha can be waged conti-
nuously. If we have discovered its real worth, we can use
this sword each time we have to fight. It is more

effective than a sword of steel. All that is required is the capacity to endure suffering. We must not fight shy of imprisonment. We must not imagine that eating mealie pap will do us any harm.

'There are persons who scoff and sneer. They say, "All this is idle talk. Whatever you do, you cannot start the campaign again. Once has been quite enough." Well, if it is true that we cannot resume the struggle, it will have been in vain that we started it at all.

'Whatever we have gained by satyagraha can be retained only through satyagraha. If satyagraha is given up, we may be sure that the gains will also be lost. If we try to retain the fruits of our victory by force, we can be crushed within the minute. Even a child can see that.

'Satyagraha is really an attitude of mind. He who has attained to the satyagrahic state of mind will remain ever victorious—at all times and places and under all conditions, whether it is a government or a people that he opposes.

'It is because we do not appreciate the marvel of satyagraha that we live in India as a poor and cowardly race, not only in our relations with the government but in our personal relations as well. Certain customs which are palpably evil are kept alive in our country mainly because we lack in the spirit of satyagraha.'

As always, Gandhi won the argument—and so it was back again to satyagraha. Hawking without licences was one of the methods. And young Harilal, Gandhi's first son, was among the first to be imprisoned. Being an

attorney, Gandhi himself could not take to hawking, but
he asked others to do so.   For his part, he would go to
court and defend those who have been arrested.

With his extraordinary courage of conviction, Gandhi
indulged   in   some   plain-speaking.   'Satyagraha,'   he
said, 'is easy for those who can understand it well. When
I go to defend those who have been arrested, I do not,
strictly speaking, defend them but only send them to jail!
If we have acquired real courage, there should be no
need for me to present myself in court.'

The proud (some might say, sadistic) father was un-
repentant at having sent his son to jail and at having
pleaded in court for the maximum penalty for the young
boy and his associates.   Said he: 'It will be a part of
Harilal's education to go to jail for the sake of the
country.   I want every Indian to do what Harilal has
done.   He is only a child and may have merely deferred
to his father's wishes.   But others should act on their
own.'

Well, well!   Here's how the court proceedings went
when our remarkable father appeared on behalf of his
20-year-old son:

> *Police sergeant:* Sir, the accused was arrested
> by me in Bellevue East for hawking fruit
> without a licence.
>
> *Gandhi:* Sir, I do not propose to call wit-
> nesses, but I wish to make a few remarks.
>
> *Magistrate:* Yes, you may.
>
> *Gandhi:* Sir, at yesterday's trial I was weak
> enough to protest against the increase of
> penalty.   In the present instance, I have
> had a long conference with the prisoner in jail

and I have been asked to request the court for the severest penalty. The accused acted in the manner he did out of deliberation. If a light sentence were imposed on him, he intends, as soon as he comes out of jail, to repeat the offence. It will be a saving of time to give him a long sentence. Moreover, it will be better for his health if he has a sustained term!

Soon the jail was getting filled again. Some one hundred Indians had gone in, come out and gone in again. No fines were, of course, paid. No one pleaded not guilty. Satyagraha was back in full swing. And so were the Sunday mass meetings in the precincts of the Fordsburg mosque. Let's take a brief look at one of them.

Sunday, August 23, 1908. Out of the 13,000 Indians in the Transvaal, over 3,000 are present. Among them are Mir Alam and some of his fellow-Pathans. The meeting has scarcely begun when a dramatic note is struck by the Pathan leaders' admitting their previous errors and declaring their intention to join the fight to the bitter end. After the chairman Essop Mia has spoken, Gandhi rises to speak:

'General Smuts has told us and the world that educated Zulus and Bantus will be treated on a par with the Europeans—but not the Indians and the Chinese. If the natives of South Africa may not have the colour bar, why should the Indians and Chinese have it? Why should we have to labour under this colour disability?

'The government has hinted at the possibility of a racial conflict in this colony. In fact, a racial conflict is already going on! I do not know what the meaning of any further racial conflict may be. If it covers any threat of physical violence, I standing here before this multitude of my countrymen shall ask you to suffer even that physical injury.

'In fighting this battle with a weak people, it has not pleased General Smuts to order the jail authorities to give no hard labour to these prisoners. But no, he must fill the cup of our misery to the brim. I ask my countrymen to drink that cup if they wish to fight for a principle. I do declare that our fight—my fight—has always been for a principle, and it shall continue to be for a principle.

'General Smuts has been saying that we claim partnership. We do claim partnership. I claim it now, but I claim it as a younger brother. Their Christianity teaches them that every human being is a brother. The British constitution taught me, when yet a child, that I have equality in the eye of the law. It is purely and simply a question of time—but that equality must be given.

'Why should there be sustained cheering in the House of Parliament when General Smuts derides the idea of partnership? Yes, partnership undoubtedly. Indians will not remain in this country or in any country under the British flag as slaves. They will demand to remain in this country as men.

'General Smuts has called my private letter to him an ultimatum! Nonsense! There was no such intention. I ask the government and the colonists to trust us.

We will play the game. But let us not be called upon to wear the bar sinister.'

The meeting ended with several hundred more registration certificates—apparently belonging to doubting Thomases within the Indian community—being consigned to the fire.

As was his wont, Gandhi also took up the fight with the local press. 'It is wonderful,' he wrote to the *Rand Daily Mail*, 'how every demand made by the British Indians is being misunderstood! Was not my claim to partnership resented? Was not its repudiation by General Smuts received with sustained cheers in the popular House? And yet, what is strange in the claim put forward by me?

'You, Sir, know well that we are taught in the public schools in India the doctrine of partnership and equality in the eye of the law. And yet, these are expressions one may not even whisper in the colony without being laughed out of court.

'If what my countrymen claim is a quibble, surely the parliament of the colony should have sufficient magnanimity to concede a quibble. The fact is that it is not a quibble. The colony wishes to establish a new principle and to draw a sharp colour line, overriding the Rhodes formula of equal rights for all civilized men south of the Zambesi. We would be less than men if we were to quietly accept such a violent departure from British tradition.'

The trend of Gandhi's argument is throughout crystal clear. But an unwary reader may miss its central point —namely, his deep conviction in the essential soundness and sincerity of the policies and professions of the British empire. It took him many, many years to eject this deep-seated conviction (one might even say, faith) from his system. But that is a long story which it is not the purpose of this book to tell.

At the same time, it would help the reader to know how Gandhi reacted to two significant events that took place in India around this time. One of these was the Muzaffarpur bomb incident of April 1908, in which the Bengal terrorist Khudiram Bose was found guilty and sentenced to death.

Commented Gandhi: 'We have no reason to rejoice at the introduction of Russian methods into India. The Indian people will not win their freedom through these methods. We have no reason to believe that what is effective in Russia will be efficacious for India too.

'It is likely that these incidents will distract people from their duty. The easy and straightforward methods of campaigning for one's rights will be gradually eschewed and, in the end, the methods which we imagine we would use only against foreigners will be used against ourselves. This has ever been so.'

Here we have a faint glimpse of how Gandhi began his long-distance selling of satyagraha to the Indian people, long before he himself became a part of the Indian political scene.

The other incident related to Tilak's articles in the *Kesari*, praising the work of the Bengal revolutionaries, and his subsequent arrest and deportation. Gandhi's comment on this is again typical of how his mind was working.

He wrote: 'Mr. Tilak is so great a man and scholar that it would be impertinent to write of his work. Yet we should not blindly follow the policies of those whom we regard as great. It would be casting a reflection on Mr. Tilak's greatness to argue that his writings had no bitterness in them. Pungent, bitter and penetrating writing was his objective. He aimed at inciting Indians against British rule.

'From their point of view, the rulers are justified in taking action against such a man. We would do the same in their place. However, Mr. Tilak deserves our congratulations. By his suffering he has laid the foundations of India's freedom.'

Then Gandhi returns to his leitmotif: 'India's welfare does not consist in merely uprooting British rule. It will be harmful, even useless, to use force or violence for uprooting that rule. Freedom gained through violence would not endure. The masses would merely pass from one form of slavery to another.

'The easiest way to make British rule beneficent is to adopt the way of satyagraha. If British rule becomes tyrannical, it will come to an end as soon as it attempts to resist satyagraha.

'What is our duty in this context? Mr. Tilak differs from us, but we must emulate his capacity to suffer. His object is the same as ours, namely, to serve the motherland and to work for its prosperity. But we are concerned that the outcome of our exertions will be a thousand times better.'

Meanwhile many Indian satyagrahis were having a horrendous time in jail. The case of Syed Ali is an example. Reporting this, Gandhi wrote: 'It is becoming more certain each day that we shall be made to drain the cup of misery to its dregs. Mr. Syed Ali was made to carry closet buckets. He was made to stay in cold water for a long spell. He was kicked. How can one bear this?

'Nevertheless, we will carry buckets and suffer kicks. We will regard this as an expression of our nobility. Our bonds will be loosened when we enjoy carrying buckets. Only then may we claim to have understood the meaning of satyagraha.'

Within ten days of writing this, Gandhi himself was arrested and sent to Volksrust jail. It was almost ten months to the day when he first suffered incarceration in Johannesburg. Of course, 'suffered' is hardly the word. Although this was his second imprisonment, jails had already become something like a holiday home for Gandhi. He nicknamed the Volksrust jail 'King Edward's Hotel' and one of the first things he did was to write to Doke.

Doke had written to him only a few days earlier. He was then engaged in writing Gandhi's biography and he was bursting with queries of all kinds. Said Doke: 'Try and not get confiscated and deported or anything of that kind, if you can help it just now. I have a thousand questions to ask—on any one of which, of course, the welfare of the British empire depends! Especially, I want a good cabinet photograph of yourself—without your hat. So don't get caught.'

Gandhi's short reply was a model of unflappability. 'The expected has happened,' he wrote, 'and I think it is as well. I have arrived just in time. You will say I have accepted the hospitality before the "settings" were finished. I think it was better that I should do that than that the invitation should be rejected for the sake of the "settings".... I must stop now as I have been called away to give digit impressions.'

Thus began Gandhi's second momentous sojourn in prison. He had just completed his thirty-ninth birthday. There were some forty of his compatriots along with him.

Here is a first impression, bubbling with typical Gandhian humour, of 'King Edward's Hotel'. 'Indians are so happy here,' reported Gandhi, 'that one should think of it as a palace. It is well built, constructed of stone. The cells are large and ventilation is satisfactory. For bathing there are three showers. Water pours out of these in large quantities, enabling one to have a very good bath.'

Try as he might, Gandhi found no time in prison either to answer Doke's numerous questions or provide him with materials relating to the Indian struggle in South Africa, for incorporation in the book Doke was then writing. 'In your leisure moments from hard labour,' Doke had urged Gandhi, 'try and note down all you can remember step by step.' But it was easier said than done.

However, Gandhi did succeed in sending Doke, at his request, a message to the youth of India. This has an important bearing on what I am trying to say in this book. I shall therefore quote it in full: 'I am not sure,' wrote Gandhi, 'that I have any right to send a message to those with whom I have never come into personal contact.   But it has been desired, and I consent.   These then are my thoughts.

'The struggle in the Transvaal is not without its interest for India. We are engaged in raising men who will give good account of themselves in any part of the world.

'We have undertaken the struggle on the following assumptions: (a) Passive resistance is always infinitely superior to physical force. (b) There is no inherent barrier between Europeans and Indians anywhere. (c) Whatever may have been the motives of the British rulers in India, there is a desire on the part of the nation at large to see that justice is done.

'It would be a calamity to break the connection between the British people and the people of India. If we are treated as, or assert our right to be treated as, free men, whether in India or elsewhere, the connection between the British people and the people of India cannot only be mutually beneficial, but is calculated to be of enormous advantage to the world religiously and, therefore, socially and politically.   In my opinion each nation is the complement of the other.

'Passive resistance, in connection with the Transvaal struggle, I should hold justifiable on the strength of any of these propositions. It may be a slow remedy, but I regard it as an absolutely sure remedy, not only for our ills in the Transvaal but for all the political and other troubles from which our people suffer in India.'

Let us pause awhile over this statement.   Let us note, in particular, the absolute confidence and certainty with which Gandhi puts forward his propositions.   And the propositions themselves, if understood correctly, show the unmistakable direction in which Gandhi's mind is working.

What is this direction? First of all he looks upon the struggle in the Transvaal not as an end in itself but as providing the training ground for things to come. In other words, he is already preparing himself (if not also his closest colleagues) for that return to India which has been his most deeply cherished goal almost from the very beginning. For, without doubt, India would provide him with the final proving ground for his revolutionary idea of satyagraha. Its success in the Transvaal would mean little: it had to succeed in India.

Secondly, he is convinced that the British connection is not all that bad as most of his countrymen—and particularly some of the top Indian leaders—make it out to be. Indeed, he would be happy if the connection continued for ever. This is the kind of apologia that can be easily misunderstood. It does look as though Gandhi is defending the British empire. But is he?

Here we come to the crux of what I shall call the Gandhi problem. In this statement I see a first glimmer of what it is that Gandhi is buckling up to fight. Not the British empire, but something of which it is but a symptom, something which lies lurking behind the facade of politics and power. It is towards the discovery of that root disease that Gandhi's mind is moving. And it is towards the revelation of Gandhi's discovery that this book is primarily and substantively orientated.

But the time for that revelation is not yet. We must build up towards it very gradually. We must linger, for a further space of time, over the traumata. For without these, Gandhi's discovery would have remained at the level of abstraction, a mere idea, unclothed in flesh and blood and, therefore, incapable of setting the world on fire.

Gandhi's second experience of life in the South African jails lasted a little over two months. He has left behind a searing account of the experience, so that we are able to get a grand-stand view of the process by which prophets are made.

Prefacing the account, Gandhi writes: 'A campaign of satyagraha can take many forms, but it is found that jail-going is the most effective means of fighting political disabilities. I think we shall have to go to jail often enough—and not only during the present agitation, but for fighting future disabilities. Every Indian should therefore know all that is worth knowing about jail-life.'

Gandhi's almost congenital anxiety to get into jail is worth a thought. 'I was much worried,' he writes, 'lest the case against me should be withdrawn. The magistrate retired for some time after the other cases had been disposed of. This made me all the more nervous. Eventually the magistrate returned and my case was called out. I was then sentenced to a fine of 25 pounds or to two months' hard labour. This made me very happy. I congratulated myself on what I considered to be my good fortune in being allowed to join the others in jail.'

Before the sentence was passed, Gandhi made a statement. 'As an officer of this court,' he said, 'I owe an explanation. There have been differences between the government and the British Indians whom I represent. After due deliberation, I took upon myself the responsibility of advising my countrymen not to submit to the primary obligation imposed by the Asiatic Act but, as law-abiding citizens, to accept its sanctions. Rightly or wrongly, I consider that the Act offends our conscience and that the only way we could show our feeling was to incur its penalties. I am now before the court to suffer the penalties that may be awarded to me.'

The prosecutor argued that as Gandhi had admitted his sin to be greater than that of the others, he should be awarded the heaviest penalty, namely, a fine of one hundred pounds or three months' hard labour.

In giving judgement, the magistrate said how very sorry he was to see attorney Gandhi in the dock, but that he had to make a difference between him and the others (who had been given lighter penalties) since his job was simply to administer the law.

Rigorous imprisonment, of which this was Gandhi's first experience, meant nine hours of hard labour. Woken up sharp at a half past five in the morning, the prisoners are expected to be ready to march out to the work-site by six o'clock. At seven the work starts. 'On the first day,' narrates Gandhi, 'we had to dig up the soil in a field near the main road. We were taken there along with the Kaffirs. The soil was very hard, and since it had to be dug up with spades, the labour involved was strenuous. The day was very hot. We set to work with great energy but, unused as most of us were to hard work, we were soon quite exhausted.

'As the day advanced, we found the task even harder. The warder was rather sharp of temper. He shouted at the prisoners all the time to keep on working. The

more he shouted, the more nervous the Indians became.
I saw some of them in tears. One, I noticed, had a
swollen foot. I was sorely distressed at this. However,
I went on urging everyone to ignore the warder and
carry on as best as he could.

'Soon I too was exhausted. There were large blisters
on the palms, the lymph oozing out of them. It was
difficult to bend down, and the spade seemed to weigh
a maund. All the time I was praying to God to save my
honour and to give me strength to keep doing the work
as well as I should.

'Placing my trust in Him, I went on with the work.
The warder started rebuking me, when I rested for a
while. I told him there was no need to shout at me and
that I would do my best and work to the utmost limit of
my endurance.

'Just then I saw Mr. Jhinabhai Desai fainting away.
I paused a little, not being allowed to leave the place of
work. The warder went to the spot. I found that I
too must go, and I ran. Two other Indians followed me.
Water was sprinkled over Jhinabhai. He came to.
The warder sent away the others to their work. I was
allowed to remain by his side. After plenty of coldwater
had been poured over his head, he felt somewhat better.

'Sitting by Jhinabhai, I thought to myself: "A great
many Indians have been going to jail at my word.
What a sinner would I be if I had been giving wrong
advice! Am I the cause of all this suffering?"

'As I thought thus, I sighed deeply. I considered the
matter afresh, with God as witness. After being plunged
in reflection for some time, I collected myself with a smile.
I felt I had given the right advice. If to bear suffering is

in itself a kind of happiness, there is no cause for worry. After all, this was only a case of fainting, but even if it were to be death, I could have given no other advice. I felt light in heart and tried to instil courage in him.'

The work-site where Gandhi underwent his first day of hard labour was within close view of the market square in Volksrust and about a mile and a half from the jail. Many passers-by were therefore eye-witnesses of what was going on. The incident, naturally, blew up into a public scandal. Questions were asked in the House of Commons in London. A Reuter cable said: 'The Indians who were sentenced yesterday, including Mr. Gandhi, were today working on the market square here at road making.' Doke, in a letter to a fellow minister, said: 'Mr. Gandhi was sentenced last Wednesday to two months' imprisonment with hard labour and may now be seen in prison clothes, with a pick-axe, road-making in Volksrust market place, in company with the Kaffir gang.' But amidst this hullabaloo, when interviewed by the Reuter correspondent, Gandhi said he was the happiest man in the Transvaal!

The *Rand Daily Mail* carried an angry letter of protest against the treatment meted out to Gandhi. Parts of the letter are worth quoting:

'If President Kruger sent Mr. Gandhi and other high-class Indians in prison garb to break stones on the public roads of the late republic, for no better reason than that they have been convicted, it would lead to an ultimatum from the British government, which would put a stop to it in twenty-four hours.

'Yet this British colony of eighteen months old, which has scarcely shed its political swaddling clothes, does it with impunity. Mr. Gandhi's crime which he is expiating by breaking stones on the streets of Volksrust, in a dress ornamented with broad arrows, is practically a protest against these odious laws.

'Mr. Gandhi comes of the same class as the Prime Minister of Nepal, who has lately been the honoured guest of England. He is a man of high educational attainments, a barrister of the Inns of Court and a man of high moral character and an exemplary life. And yet, to such a man, the Transvaal laws offer the same insult.'

Ratanshi Sodha, who was among Gandhi's fellow labourers on that traumatic day, supplements the narration of events vividly: 'We were taken out to work on the side of the agricultural show ground, close to the fence which divides it from the public road. Our work there was to dig and remove stones. We were quite close to the road, and anybody who passed by could easily see us and hear distinctly what was going on.

'The European warder who was in charge of the Indian prisoners kept on urging Mr. Gandhi to work harder and harder, though Mr. Gandhi was doing his best. All this might have been heard by the passersby clearly. The exact words were: "Come on, Gandhi. Come on, Gandhi." The warder kept urging him when he saw him stoop to pick up earth to rub on the palms of his hands, which were getting raw through blistering.

'When after nine hours of almost continuous work, Mr. Gandhi returned to the jail, he was so stiff with pain and fatigue that he could scarcely move.

'On the next day we were taken to a piece of ground near the roadside, almost opposite Suliman Cajee's store. Mr. Cajee, who was standing in front of the store, could easily see and hear whatever was going on. We were digging holes for trees and worked, as on the previous day, for nine hours.'

A careful reader will have noticed the difference in emphasis in the accounts given by Gandhi and Sodha. Gandhi scarcely refers to the humiliation of being seen at work, in convict's garb, by passers-by. To him, it was an exercise in self-flagellation and a source of joy rather than sorrow. It was his *yajna*, a ceremony of innocence—or rather, the ritualistic process by which a *dvija* enters his second birth.

Let alone the humiliation, the work itself—how best you do it—was to Gandhi the core of his *yajna*. It was his way of reducing the *Bhagavad-gita* to action. And far from condemning his oppressors, it was upon his own fellow-prisoners that his critical eye was turned. Shirkers, he called them roundly.

'It is my confirmed belief,' he reflects, 'that we get a bad name because of this habit of shirking work, and it is one of the reasons that our struggle is being prolonged. Satyagraha is a difficult as well as an easy method. Our bona fides must not be in doubt. We bear no ill will towards the government. We do not regard it as our enemy. If we are fighting it, it is with a view to correcting its errors and making it mend its ways. We would not be happy to see it in difficulties. Even our resistance is for its good.

'It follows from this line of reasoning, that we at any rate should work to the best of our ability in jail.

It does not become us to be lazy or to shirk work. As satyagrahis, it is our duty to do whatever work is given to us.

'In every cell, it is the duty of the prisoners to carry the urine bucket placed in it. I observed that our people are unwilling to do such work. In fact, there is no reason that one should mind it. It is wrong to think of any work as humiliating or degrading. Moreover, those who have offered themselves for imprisonment cannot afford to stand on prestige. I saw that sometimes there was argument as to who should carry the bucket.

'If we have understood the full meaning of satyagraha, we would compete with one another in offering to do such work. Instead of making difficulties about it, one should feel honoured if the work fell to one's lot.

'Since we have resolved to bear all suffering, he who suffers most should feel most honoured. An example of this was set by Mr. Hassan Mirza. Delicate of health and suffering from a disease of the lungs, he gladly took upon himself whatever work fell to his lot from day to day, without giving any thought to his health. Once a Kaffir warder asked him to clean the chief warder's privy, which he instantly started doing. As he had never done such work before, he vomited. But he was not upset by this. While he was cleaning another privy, I happened to pass by. I was astonished. To be sure, I felt great affection for him.

'On another occasion, the same Kaffir warder was ordered by his chief to find two Indians to clean the latrines specially set apart for them. The warder approached me about this and asked me to name two persons. I thought I was the best person for such work, and so I went myself. Personally I feel no shame in this kind of work. I think we should accustom ourselves to it. If we are hurt by the nature of the work assigned to us, we cannot take part in any fight worth the name.'

After nearly three weeks, Gandhi was suddenly taken away from the Volksrust jail to Johannesburg. The reason was that he was required there to give evidence in a trial. Not knowing the real reason, speculation ran high among his fellow-prisoners. 'Everyone was filled with hope,' narrates Gandhi, 'and imagined that perhaps there might be an interview with General Smuts!'

'A warder was specially sent from Johannesburg to fetch me. A railway compartment was placed at our disposal. I was in jail uniform throughout the journey. I had some luggage with me, which I was made to carry myself. The distance from the jail to the station had to be covered on foot.

'After arriving at Johannesburg, I had to reach the jail on foot, carrying the luggage myself. The incident provoked strong comments in newspapers. Questions were again asked in the British parliament. Many persons felt hurt. Everyone thought that, being a political prisoner, I should not have been made to walk the distance, dressed in jail uniform and carrying a load.'

Here is an eye-witness account of the whole bizarre exhibition: 'The train carrying Gandhi arrived at Park Station at six o'clock in the evening. Carrying his bundle of clothes in a large bag marked with the broad arrow, a basket of books and, of course, wearing the convict suit, Gandhi was then marched in custody from the station to the Fort. It was then broad daylight and the streets were filled with onlookers, some of whom recognized him even in the hideous guise that he wore.'

The government tried to slur over the incident and to defend its action by suggesting that when the train arrived it was already rather dark. Polark declared in an affidavit that this was a brazen lie: 'The train arrived at the scheduled time, namely six o'clock. The sun did not set until a considerable time afterwards. The official sunset time on that afternoon was 6.17 p.m. Mr. Gandhi was marched through the public streets from the station to the jail. This would take about twelve minutes. I walked part of the way at Mr. Gandhi's side. Half way to the jail, I left him, walked back for about ten minutes to catch my train, and thereafter went home. When I reached home it was still daylight, approaching dusk.'

In a letter to the press, the incensed Polak hit out at the government mercilessly: 'Is there any excuse for bringing Mr. Gandhi from Volksrust to Johannesburg in convict garb and marching him from Park Station to the Fort in full public view. I believe that when the Spanish Inquisition desired to degrade its victims, among whom were probably ancestors of mine (Polak, it will be recalled, was a Jew) it clothed them in bag-shaped yellow garb and marched them in this fashion through the streets, prior to despatching them at the customary *auto-da fe*. We Transvaal Britishers do not seem to have gone far beyond those mediaeval torturers in our desire to bring our victims to what, in our opinion, is a fitter frame of mind! It makes one flush with shame to think of it all.'

The uproar forced the hands of the government to some extent. For on a later occasion, in another bout of incarceration, Gandhi was brought from the Pretoria jail to the magistrate's court in civilian clothes—but handcuffed! Never before had he been subjected to this particular kind of humiliation.

Doke was flabbergasted. In controlled anger, he wrote in the *Rand Daily Mail*: 'Of course there may be amongst us those who will be glad to hear that indignities are being heaped on this great Indian leader. But I venture to hope that the great majority of our colonies will feel ashamed and angry that a man of the character and position of Mr. Gandhi should be needlessly insulted in this way.

'He came voluntarily from Natal to be imprisoned. He has always shown the utmost chivalry in his dealings with the authorities. Why then should shameful indignities be put upon him?'

A letter in *The Transvaal Leader* exposed the vulgarity even more pointedly. The writer said: 'I am not aware that the prison regulations demand that a prisoner, when giving evidence in court, should in all circumstances be handcuffed. If it is a fact that a man like Mr. Gandhi—one of the quietest and most unassuming men going, highly educated, and a gentleman to the tips of his fingers—was handcuffed and submitted to that unnecessary indignity, it seems to me monstrous and nothing short of a shame and a disgrace.'

When the handcuffs question was raised in the House of Commons, the government reply was typically vague. 'There has been no suggestion,' said the spokesman (evidently with tonque is cheek,) 'that Mr. Gandhi has been subjected to any special disability. He has been treated in every respect as any other prisoner would have been treated. And on a previous occasion he himself said he did not wish to be treated in any other way!'

The burlesque is complete when we read what the Transvaal Prime Minister's minute on the subject says: 'Mr. Gandhi was however allowed to draw his sleeves over his handcuffs and to carry a book, which concealed the fact of his being handcuffed!'

Against this public uproar and government double-talk, look at Gandhi's own comment: 'There is no reason that one should feel these things so much. It is not likely that in this country the government will make any distinction between political and other prisoners. The greater the harassment we suffer, the earlier shall we win our release. Moreover, we shall find on reflection that it is not much of a hardship to have to wear a jail uniform, or go on foot carrying one's luggage, or wear handcuffs.'

To resume Gandhi's narrative about his sudden transfer from Volksrust to Johannesburg: 'It was evening when we reached Johannesburg. I was not taken to where I could be among other Indians, but was given a bed in a cell of the prison where there were mostly Kaffir prisoners who had been lying ill. I spent the night in this cell in great misery and fear. Thinking that I would be kept in this place all the time, I became quite nervous. I felt extremely uneasy, but I resolved in my mind that my duty required me to bear

71

every suffering. I read the *Bhagavad-gita* which I had carried with me. I read the verses which had a bearing on my situation. I meditated on them and thus managed to compose myself.

'The reason that I felt so uneasy was that the Kaffir and Chinese prisoners appeared to be wild, murderous and given to immoral ways. Nor did I know their language. When a Kaffir started putting questions to me, I felt he was mocking me. I did not understand what he was saying and returned no reply. Then he asked me in broken English why I had been brought there in that fashion. I gave a brief reply, and then I lapsed into silence.

'Then came a Chinese. He appeared to be worse. He came near the bed and looked closely at me. I kept still. Then he went to a Kaffir lying in bed. The two exchanged obscene jokes, uncovering each other's genitals. Both these prisoners had charges of murder and larceny against them. Knowing this, how could I possibly sleep?

'Real suffering lies in this. Carrying luggage and such other troubles are nothing very serious. We may entertain no aversion to Kaffirs, but we cannot ignore the fact that there is no common ground between them and us in the daily affairs of life.

'I had one further unpleasant experience. In this jail the avatories have open access. There are no doors. One morning, as soon as I had occupied one of them, there came along a strong, well-built, fearful-looking Kaffir. He asked me to get out and started abusing me. I said I would leave very soon. Instantly he lifted me up in his hands and threw me out. Fortunately, I caught hold of the door-frame and saved myself from a fall. I was not in the least frightened by what happened. I smiled and walked away. But one or two Indian prisoners who were around started weeping. As for myself, I had no motions for four days!

'The freedom from some regulations, which was permitted in Volksrust, was impossible in Johannesburg. For instance, when prisoners first come to jail they are examined by the physician. This is done in order to isolate anyone suffering from a contagious disease. Some prisoners are found to suffer from syphilis, and therefore everyone has to have his genitals examined. For this purpose, the prisoners are totally undressed while being examined. Kaffirs are kept standing naked for nearly 15 minutes so as to save the physician's time.

'Indian prisoners are made to lower their breeches only when the physician approaches them. The other garments have to be removed in advance. Almost every Indian resents having to lower his breeches, but most of them co-operate in the routine procedure so as not to harm our movement, although at heart they feel ill at ease.

'When in the presence of men only, there should be no need to conceal any parts of our anatomy. There is no reason to believe that others will keep staring at the parts which we generally hide. We need not have any false sense of shame. If we are pure in our own minds, where is the need to be particular about hiding what is a part of our natural endowment?'

After ten days, Gandhi was brought back to the

Volksrust jail. 'I was dressed in the prisoners' uniform,' he recounts, 'but instead of being made to walk to the railway station, I was taken in a cab. By way of provisions for the journey, I was given half a pound of bread and bully-beef. I refused the latter.

'When I reached the station, I found some Indian tailors present. They noticed me. Of course, talking was not allowed. Observing my dress, some of them were filled with tears. Since I was not free even to tell them that I did not mind my dress, I remained a silent spectator.

'On reaching Volksrust, I was again made to walk the distance from the station to the jail and carry my luggage. All the Indian prisoners were happy to find me back amongst them.

'Since Indians of all communities and castes lived together in the jail, it gave me an opportunity to observe how backward we are in the matter of self-government. At the same time, we were not altogether incapable of self-government either, for whatever difficulties cropped up were always overcome in the end.

'Some Hindus said they were not prepard to take food cooked by Muslims or by certain individuals. Men who hold such views should never stir out of India. I also observed that no objection was raised if any Kaffir or white touched our food!

'It so happened once that someone objected to sleeping near a certain person, on the ground that the latter belonged to the scavenger caste. On probing deeper into the matter, it was found that the objection was raised not because he minded it himself but because he was afraid of being declared an outcaste should members of his community in India come to hear of it!

'Thanks to these hypocritical distinctions of high and low, we have turned our backs on truth and embraced falsehood. How can we be called satyagrahis if, knowing that it is wrong to despise the scavenger, we still do so out of an unreasonable fear of ostracism at home?

'I wish that Indians who join this movement should also resort to satyagraha against their caste and family or wherever evil is found. It is because we do not act in this way that the successful outcome of our struggle is being delayed. How can we Indians cling to false distinctions among ourselves and, at the same time, demand our rights as a single community?'

Before we come to the end of this account of Gandhi's second experience of jail life, let us see what he read during his two month's incarceration. 'Though I had limited time, since the entire day was taken up with work,' writes Gandhi, 'I managed to read two books by Ruskin, the essays of Thoreau, some portions of the Bible, a life of Garibaldi, and Bacon's essays, besides two books about India. We can find the doctrine of satyagraha in the writings of Ruskin and Thoreau. I also read the *Bhagavad-gita* almost every day. All this reading had the effect of confirming my belief in satyagraha. Life in jail is not in the least boring.'

Some of the horrifying experiences which Gandhi had to undergo in jail may appear differently to different readers. Some may see in them merely the over-reaction of an over-sensitive soul. Others may see in them manifestations of timidity and an inhibited psyche. But if I have ploughed through them with such care, it is because I find in them the traumata out of which a prophet is fashioned.

But the story of Gandhi's greatest trial has yet to be told. Out of this trial he emerges with a triumph that passes all understanding. Now he is at once prophet, saint and seer—although, to anyone's surprise, we find him dismissing the incident with a rather low-key epithet. He calls it simply 'a moral dilemma'.

'When I had completed about half the term of my imprisonment, writes Gandhi, 'there was a telegram from Phoenix to say that my wife was seriously ill and that I should go down there immediately. Everyone was grieved, but I had no doubt as to my duty. When the jailer asked me whether I would agree to pay the fine to obtain my release, I replied without the slightest hesitation that I would never do so and that it was implied in our movement that we should bear separation from our kith and kin. At this the jailer smiled sadly.'

The telegram was from West, who was managing things at the Phoenix settlement in Natal during Gandhi's absence. Replying to the telegram, Gandhi wrote: 'It cuts me but does not surprise me. It is impossible for me to leave here unless I pay the fine— which I will not. When I embarked upon the struggle I counted the cost. If Mrs. Gandhi must leave me without even the consolation a devoted husband could afford, so be it.'

Kasturba was suffering from haemorrhage and her condition was grave.

Gandhi went on: 'Please do what you all can for her. I am wiring Harilal to go there. I expect from you or

someone a daily bulletin—not that I can help thereby.
Please let me know by wire what the disease is exactly. I
am enclosing a letter for her. I hope she will be alive
and conscious to receive and understand the letter. Let
Manilal read it to her.'

The letter Gandhi enclosed for Kasturba is a fascinating document. It says: 'The news about your illness
cuts my heart, but I am not in a position to go there to
nurse you. I have offered my all to the satyagraha
struggle. My coming there is out of the question. I
can only come if I pay the fine—which I must not.

'If you keep courage and take the necessary nutrition,
you will recover. If however my ill-luck so has it that
you pass away, I should only say that there would be
nothing wrong in it, separated though you would be
from me while I am still alive. I love you so dearly that
even if you are dead, you will be alive to me. Your soul
is deathless.

'I repeat what I have frequently told you. I assure
you that, if you do succumb to your illness, *I will not marry
again*.

'Time and again have I told you that you may quietly
breathe your last with faith in God. If you die, even
that death of yours will be a sacrifice to the cause of
satyagraha.

'My struggle is not merely political. It is religious
and therefore quite pure. It does not matter much
whether one dies in it or lives.'

What a titanic decision! In taking it Gandhi was
not unaware of the widespread misgivings it would
evoke. Reflecting on what he had done, he wrote:
'On a superficial view of the matter, this attitude would

appear to be rather harsh. But I am convinced it is the only right attitude to adopt. I think of my love for the motherland as an aspect of my religion. It is, of course, not the whole of religion. But religion cannot be considered to be complete without it.

'If necessary, we should bear separation from our family in order to be able to follow the dictates of our religion. We may even have to lose them. Not only is there no cruelty in this but it is actually our duty to do so. The history of the world is full of such instances.'

That last bit, of course, is typical of Gandhi's recourse to hyperbole. It is as untrue as his claim (repeated *ad nauseam* by others) that he had nothing new to teach the world. In his readiness to sacrifice his wife for his cause, he was either trying to imitate Harishchandra or simply displaying the one-track nature of his mind. After all, when the cry of despair reached him, it was not as though he was a thousand miles away, in the trenches. All that he had to do was pay up the fine, obtain his release and dash to his beloved wife's side. And paying the fine, in such a situation, certainly would not have meant the crack of doom for his beloved cause. But then, this is the stuff of which prophets are made!

On further reflection, I feel I have erred in describing the Kasturba episode as Gandhi's greatest trial. Nothing can try a man of his steel. He takes everything in his stride. What can you do with a man who is willing to go through everything, pay any price, for the success of his mission? If his wife is dying—let her die. If they will make him break stones—let them. If they will march him through public streets in convict dress—let them. If he is produced in court handcuffed, like a felon

—so be it. If he is thrown among murderers and exposed to sights of sexual depravity—so be it. Nothing is going to degrade him. Nothing can touch him.

Suddenly a government in despair thought it saw light. Why not isolate him from his fellow-prisoners? This would certainly bend him, even if it would not break him.

And so we come to Gandhi's third—and so far as this book is concerned, his last—experience in jail. First, it was for a month. Then it was for two months. And now he would be confined in jail for three months.

'I did not imagine,' writes Gandhi, 'that I would have much to say about this third pilgrimage to jail. But my expectation proved false. This was an altogether new kind of experience. What I have learnt from it, I could not have learnt even from years of study. In these three months I had many vivid experiences of satyagraha and, as a result, today I am a better satyagrahi than I was ever before.'

Is this another piece of Gandhian hyperbole? Let us see.

It was the Volksrust jail again. And three months' hard labour was the sentence. But Gandhi was happy as a lark among the seventy-seven other satyagrahis who were already there. For three days he went on out with the other work-gangs to quarry stone and carry them in loads to the site where a new road was being built.

But then came a telegram from the government, ordering that Gandhi should not be taken for work outside the jail compound. Naturally! Which government would relish another uproar in the House of Commons?

'I was rather disappointed,' wrote Gandhi, 'for I liked

going out. It improved my health and kept me fit. Ordinarily I have two meals a day, but on account of the exercise my stomach insisted on having three meals!'

Then came a further disappointment, for orders were received for his immediate removal to Pretoria. 'It was raining, the roads were bad. Despite this, my warder and I were obliged to leave, with my luggage on my head. I was taken by the evening train in a third-class carriage.'

In the Pretoria jail, he was put in a solitary cell. 'I began pacing up and down. Before long, the warder peeped through the watch-hole and shouted, "Gandhi, stop walking about like that. My floor is being spoiled!" I stopped and stood in a corner. I had nothing even to read.

'At eleven I was removed to another small cell. It was in this that I spent the rest of my term. It was a one-prisoner cell, measuring ten feet by seven. The floor was covered with black pitch. When the mid-day meal arrived, I had to eat it in the cell standing.'

He was under constant watch and there was not one Indian face to be seen anywhere. 'Even when I went for evacuation, a warder stood by to keep watch. If by chance he did not know me, he would shout: "Sam, come out now." But Sam had the bad habit of taking a long time for evacuation. How could he get out so soon? And if he did, how would he feel easy in bowels afterwards?

'The food was in keeping with the conditions described above. It was difficult to eat rice without ghee and I decided to give it up. For a month and a half I lived on only one midday meal of beans. I told the physician that I would certainly suffer in health if I had to go without ghee. He said in that case he would order bread for me. I thanked him, but told him that I had not approached him specially for myself. So long as ghee was not ordered for everyone, I could not accept bread.

'The same day, I was offered bread and rice. I was hungry. But, as matters stood, how could a satyagrahi accept the bread? I therefore refused both. During this month and a half my health broke down. I had lost my strength and had severe neuralgic pain in the head. I also developed symptoms of some affection in the lungs.

'I have often told satyagrahis that if anyone came out of jail with impaired health, it would be a reflection on his spirit of satyagraha. Given sufficient patience, it should be possible for us to find remedies. Moreover, one might suffer in health through worry. The satyagrahi must learn to live in jail as if it were a palace.

'I was thus anxious lest I myself should have to leave jail in poor health! However, it must be remembered that I suffered in health in the course of my satyagraha there because I could not accept ghee which had been ordered for me alone.'

Although Gandhi eventually got the jail authorities to serve ghee to all Indian prisoners, it wasn't much of an achievement, was it? In any case, the ghee helped him to recover his health sufficiently during the concluding month of his imprisonment, so that he could walk out of jail with his usual beaming smile and thus save himself the embarrassment of being looked upon by others as another all-too-human and weak-kneed satyagrahi!

What a strange man was Gandhi! Although one

cannot easily counter his thesis that in satyagraha there was no such distinction as a big issue and a small issue—yet what a fusspot he sometimes turns out to be! But then this crankishness, alas, is another of those strange ingredients that go to make a prophet.

After his final release from jail, Gandhi was on his way from Volksrust to Johannesburg by train, when at Germiston station anxious pressmen asked him about his ill-treatment. 'Oh, no' said Gandhi, 'I was very well treated. I enjoyed every minute. My complaint is against the jail regulations. The officers only did their duty in enforcing them.' In token of his gratitude, he had in fact presented a copy of Tolstoy's *The Kingdom of God is within You* to one of the warders. The inscription on the copy read: 'To Mr. G. Nelson, for his many kindnesses within the law, during my incarceration at Volksrust.'

Although, for the most part, Gandhi put on a brave face during his three successive incarcerations in 1908—covering a total of six months—he was not entirely without moments of doubt and misgiving. Of course, his anxiety concerned his fellow-satyagrahis rather than himself.

'Why should we,' he cogitated, in one such moment, 'bear such hardships, submit ourselves to the restrictions of jail life, wear coarse and ungainly dress, eat food which is hardly food, starve ourselves, suffer being kicked by the warders, live among the Kaffirs, do every kind of work whether we like it or not, obey warders who are only good enough to be our servants, be unable to receive friends or write letters, go without things that we may need, and sleep in the company if robbers and thieves? Better die than suffer all this. Better pay the fine than go to jail.

'This is one way of looking at our movement. But such an attitude will make a man quite afraid of imprisonment, and he will achieve nothing good by being in jail.

'Alternatively, one may consider oneself fortunate to be in jail in the cause of the motherland and in defence of one's honour and religion. When one is imbued with such an attitude, jail life involves no real suffering.'

So far so good. But then Gandhi goes off at a tangent and puts up a defence of jail-going which would sound hilarious to ears which are unaccustomed to his ingrained procrusteanism. His point really is a philosophical one: namely, that 'happiness and misery are states of the mind' and have little to do with one's physical situation.

'In the outside world,' argues Gandhi, 'one has to carry out the will of many, whereas in jail one has only the warder to reckon with. In jail one has no anxieties, no problem of earning one's livelihood, no worry about getting one's bread. Moreover, one's person is protected. And none of these things has to be paid for!

'By way of exercise, one gets ample work to do. And without any effort on one's part, all of one's bad habits fall away. The mind enjoys a sense of freedom. The body is held in bondage, but the soul grows more free. The body is looked after by those who hold it in bondage. Thus from every point of view, one is free in jail!

'One might perhaps be manhandled by a wicked warder, but then one learns to be patient. One feels glad to have an opportunity of dissuading him from such behaviour. It is up to us to adopt such an attitude and think of jail as a holy and happy place.'

CHILIASM

CHILIASM

Well, there we must say goodbye to 1908, the year of Gandhi's first death, the year when he became a *dvija*, the year of horror that brought to the surface both the stigmata and the traumata out of which—and out of which alone—the vision of a prophet comes to light and life. We have not looked at everything that happened in that year. That would be to deviate from the purpose of this book. Rather, we have looked at things expressionistically. We have tried—within the constraints of brevity—to lay our hands on the formative compulsions of this tempestuous twelve-month. Above all, we have tried to peek into the growth of an unusual mind which, by our pedestrian standards, is almost a freak.

Now I shall take the reader, not without trepidation, into the final act of the drama: 1909—the year of the chiliasm. To watch and meditate upon the happenings of this year is to enter the heart of Gandhi. If the significance of this twelvemonth in the life of Gandhi is missed—as it has been missed by a whole battalion of biographers, commentators and critics—we miss Gandhi altogether.

To get our story into the right focus, we need the services of a flashback. The time: Christmas day, 1896. The place: the port of Durban in South Africa. The scene: on board S.S. *Courland,* which had been lying in anchor in the port since a whole week, quarantined for no apparent reason, the yellow flag flying atop its mast. Among the passengers on board the ship are Mohandas Gandhi (age 27 years) and his family, consisting of wife and two sons.

To celebrate Christmas, the captain of the ship hosts a dinner. Convivial speeches are made after the dinner. It is now Gandhi's turn to speak. Outwardly he had taken part in the merriment, but his heart is heavy. His thoughts are in the South African struggle—not only what lay behind him but what lay ahead of him.

Hesitantly he rises to speak. 'I spoke on western civilization,' he recalls. 'I knew that this was not an occasion for a serious speech. But mine could not be otherwise. For I was the real target in the combat that was going on in Durban.

'There were two charges against me. First, that while in India on a brief six-month respite from the struggle I had indulged in unmerited condemnation of the Natal whites. Secondly, that with a view to swamping Natal with Indians I had brought shiploads of them to be settled there.

'But I was absolutely innocent. I had induced no one to go to Natal. Neither had I said, while in India, a word about the Natal whites that I had not already said in Natal itself.

'I therefore deplored the civilization of which the Natal whites were the fruit and which they represented and championed. This civilization had all along been on my mind.

'The captain and other friends gave me a patient hearing and received my speech in the spirit in which it was made. Afterwards (with the quarantine dragging on) I had long talks with the captain and other officers regarding the civilization of the West. I had in my speech described western civilization as being, unlike the eastern, predominantly based on force.

' "Ah," said the captain, "suppose the whites carry out their threat, how will you stand by your principle of nonviolence?" To which I replied: "I hope God will give me the courage to forgive them. I have no anger against them. I know that they sincerely believe that what they are doing is right and proper." '

Forward to 1909. But before we do so, let us contemplate the marvel of this young man. At 27—nay, perhaps at 25—he had already seen whither western civilization was heading. This is foresight of the first magnitude. After all, how well did he know the good and bad points of this civilization? As a student in London he had even become something of a convert to the western way of life and this relish had stuck to him for a long time thereafter. Save when in the convict's uniform, wasn't he outwardly an impeccably dressed westernized gentleman, almost beating the white man at his game?

Of course, in Natal he had seen the seamier side of the game and come face to face with a reality so ugly that any impressionable young man would be stunned into silence. What a distance from life in London—at the heart of the empire—to life on its marshy fringes in Africa and beyond. But this young man was made

of sterner stuff. Far from withdrawing into himself—
—timid and crestfallen—he was already buckling up
for a long fight. And he was not going to attack
the empire, whether at its centre or at the margins
but what lay behind the empire—the recessive mutants
of human evolution which led to such bizarre manifestations as man's inhumanity to man and, to cap it all,
man's surprising willingness (not to say docility) to
withdraw to a back seat and let the machine lead him
where it listeth.

For Gandhi, from his earliest days until the time
when many decades later his final disillusionment came,
continued to nurse a strange partiality for the empire.
During repeated interviews the South African press had
with him, at the peak of the Transvaal struggle, he continued to insist that his quarrel was with the colonial
government and not with London. Although the
evidence was at best nebulous, his faith that 'the imperial
government is with us' rarely suffered an eclipse. When
hard pressed, he would argue: 'Well, I have so great
a faith in the spirit of our struggle that even before the
imperial government intervenes, all the colonies of
South Africa will say, "No, we must grant those just
demands." There are already signs of that in the
Transvaal.'

There could be no arguing round a man of such
faith. He once went to the extent of expressing his
belief 'that the fullest expansion of national sentiment is
quite consistent with the stability of British rule in
India' and that if there was any unreasonable agitation
after legitimate demands had been met, 'I would
become a passive resister against my own countrymen'.
The implication of these sentiments is plain. The

imperial connection was important and nothing should be done, outside the bounds of national self-respect, to weaken it.

This explains, at least partly, his unfailing readiness to pack off to London if there was the faintest chance— what plainly looked like a mirage to others less pre-disposed—that the imperial government could be brought to pressurize its South African colonies to concede the Indian demand for equity and justice.

And so, on to London—in many ways the city nearest to Gandhi's heart. In all he had been here five times. This was his third visit, and the second as a member of a deputation. After going through the hell and brimstone of almost a year and a half of prison life, to be able to reconcile oneself to such a step is in itself an achievement of no mean order. Of course, in his idyll of satyagraha, ' the grim prisons of Johannesburg, Pretoria, Heidelberg and Volksrust are like the four gateways to the garden of God '. Describe the garden, please. ' Self-restraint, unselfishness, patience, gentleness—these are the flowers which spring beneath the feet of those who accept, but refuse to impose, suffering.'

Monday, June 21, 1909. Eleven in the morning. Park Station was crowded with Indians, many of them with bouquets and garlands. Every face was lit up with hope.

The train reached Cape Town half an hour late. On board the ship were two cables of greetings from fellow-satyagrahis. Gandhi reads them and is touched to the quick. One says: ' Suffering in jail for country's

6 **91**

sake preferable to going with you.   Wish you success.'
The other: 'On way to jail, wish the deputation
success.   Can serve the community best through jail.'

Of course Gandhi has no illusions.   He reflects:
'There can be nothing but empty bubbles where we
are going.   Those who are in jail are assuredly serving
the community.   Whatever the deputation may be
able to achieve will be nothing as compared to the
value of their service.'

Some three years ago, Gandhi had gone to London on
a similar deputation.   Of course it had led nowhere.
But he discerns a slight difference between then and
now.   'In 1906,' he ruminates, 'although the Indian
community had pledged itself to go to jail, no one was
sure who would do so.   Now we know of men who are
saturated with love of jail-going.   Now we, as well as
the whole world, know our latent strength.   The
prisoners prove to the world that the Indians have
grown to be men.

'The prisoners are the strong limb of the Indian
community, while the deputation is the debilitated
one.   Those who have gone to jail have nothing to
be disappointed about, while those who have pinned
their hopes on the deputation will be disappointed if
it returns empty-handed.'

As the *Kenilworth Castle* steams out to sea, Gandhi
lapses into a mood of self-denigration.   'Our enemies
are uniting,' he laments, 'but no one comes forward
to say that we Indians must also unite.   That is the
real solution.   Ignoring that, Indians have been
begging for something to be brought to them from
England as a gift.   This shows our utter helplessness.
The whites of the colonies are the strong and favoured

sons of the empire. We are the weak and neglected ones. How can we get a hearing? By petitioning? Impossible. A petition must have sanctions behind it. It must be equivalent to a polite command.'

On the high seas each day passes without any perceptible excitement and Gandhi falls deeper into despondency. The deputation—of course to keep up its status—is travelling first-class. But the horror of it all sinks into his sensitive soul. ' We are being looked after like babies,' he cries out in despair. ' There is something to eat every two hours. We cannot even lift a glass of water with our own hands. At table, it is bad manners to reach out one's hand for a spoon lying at some distance.

' It vexes me to observe the present state of my hands and compare it with what they were like in jail. I envy the servants at their work. I have neither the peace nor the freedom I enjoyed in jail. I live hedged in on all sides. My prayers lack the depth, the serenity and the concentration they had when I was in jail.

' Those who wish to serve God cannot afford to pamper themselves. Prayers do not come easily in an atmosphere of luxury. You cannot escape its natural influence upon you. This is not to suggest that we must spend all our life in jail. But we would certainly profit by the simplicity and solitude we find there.'

Most of the time Gandhi spent in reading—and of course drafting the statement on ' The British Indian Case in the Transvaal '. He lived frugally, eating only two meals a day. Don't look about for a list of the things he avoided eating! ' As my body hardens,' he reflected, ' I am growing more convinced every day that I can do with still simpler food. On this voyage I do not feel a craving for delicacies as I did on the previous occasion.'

The statement, as finally published in London, is a rather long document of forty-two paragraphs. Ampthill made several constructive emendations, one of which considerably mollified the wording of the statement's conclusion. Gandhi had spoken here of the role of the imperial government in somewhat harsh terms, accusing it of 'shirking its duty'. This will not do, said Ampthill. At this stage of the negotiations, it was in the interests of the deputation to be as conciliatory as possible.

The conclusion, as amended, read: 'Apart from any promise made by General Smuts, it is submitted that the two Indian demands are intrinsically just, that it is not difficult for the government to grant them, and that in order to have them granted the Transvaal Indians have gone through a long course of sustained suffering. In the circumstances, they feel that their covenant should be respected and that regard for the wishes of the self-governing colonies should not debar the imperial government from protecting British subjects in the same way as it would protect them in foreign countries—the more so when such subjects are unrepresented, as in the present instance.'

While still at sea, back home in South Africa there occurred the tragic death of Sammy Nagappen, a young satyagrahi, as a result of ill-treatment in jail. Gandhi called Nagappen's martyrdom the first sacrifice and brooded over it in great anguish. He lost no time in mentioning the tragedy in a footnote to the statement. The footnote read: 'Since preparing the foregoing statement, the delegates have received a telegram which shows that an Indian youth named Nagappen, imprisoned for ten days with hard labour, was discharged in a dying condition and died soon after. The allegations are that it was bitterly cold, insufficient blankets were supplied, the warders were brutal and medical attendance was not forthcoming.'

Nagappen's death weighed so heavily on Gandhi's mind that it chased him around during his stay in London. In a letter to Polak, who was then in India as a one-man delegation pleading the South African Indian cause, he wrote: 'You will have received Nagappen's photograph. I wish you could get the papers there to reproduce it. I have suggested to our people in Johannesburg to found a Nagappen scholarship. If there is anybody in Bombay or Madras who would do so, it would be very striking. Let them realize that a youth of twenty, of unblemished character, had died for the sake of his country.'

He also took up the matter with the London press: ' I venture to think that we have a right to expect you to support us, give due publicity to the movement, and favour it with your advocacy, regard being had to the fact that nearly fifty per cent of the present Indian population of the Transvaal have passed through its jails and that one young Indian has succumbed to pneumonia, caught by him whilst in jail.'

And he spoke about it in public meetings: 'The British public should know what our struggle has meant to us. Half of our people has already been to jail, of whom one young man died of pneumonia contracted in jail. Fathers and sons have together gone to jail. Mothers have taken up baskets and sold fruit in the streets to support themselves and their children while their husbands were in jail.'

Almost as soon as the deputation landed in Southampton, or very soon thereafter, Gandhi sensed that they had come at the wrong time. 'For the present,' he reported, 'we are refraining from giving information to newspapers. It is Lord Ampthill's advice that we should not. Very bad time, too, to seek interviews with the public figures here. Everyone is out of town on holiday. Moreover, the British people are preoccupied with their own affairs. The new budget has raised a storm in parliament. Also the visit of the South African statesmen [Botha, Smuts, et al] makes a heavy demand on people's time. Considering all this and looking at the circumstances around us, I am inclined to believe that, should the private moves that are under way at present fail, nothing is likely to be achieved by our visit.'

Something worse had happened in London, even before their arrival, to pollute the atmosphere. This was the assassination of Curzon Wyllie by an Indian student, Madanlal Dhingra. The two deaths that ushered in the deputation's arrival—Nagappen, a martyr, and Wyllie, a sort of hostage—occurred within days of each other.

Wyllie was Morley's aide-de-camp and had served before in India. The assassination took place at a tea party, organized by the National Indian Association of London with the object of bringing Indian students into contact with Englishmen. Wyllie was one of the guests. Reports Gandhi in anger: 'From this point of view Dhingra murdered his guest in his own house!'

He goes on: 'It is being said in defence of the assassination that it is the British who are responsible for India's ruin and that it is the right of any Indian to kill any Englishman. Every Indian should reflect on the murder. It has done India much harm. The deputation's efforts have also received a setback, though this need not be taken into consideration.

'Dhingra's defence is inadmissible. He has acted like a coward. One can only pity him. He was egged on to do this act by ill-digested reading of worthless writings. His defence appears to have been learnt by rote. It is those who incited him that deserve to be punished. In my view, Dhingra himself is innocent. The murder was committed in a state of intoxication. A mad idea, when it takes hold of one, can banish the fear of death. Whatever courage there is in Dhingra's act is the result of intoxication and not a quality of the man himself. Real courage consists in suffering deeply and over a long period.

'Those who argue that such murders may do good to India are ignorant men indeed. No act of treachery can ever profit a nation. Even should the British leave in consequence of such murderous acts, who will rule in their places? The murderers, of course.

'Is the Englishman bad because he is an Englishman? Is it that everyone with an Indian skin is good? No, India can gain nothing from the rule of murderers—no matter whether they are black or white. Under such a rule, India will be utterly ruined and laid waste.'

What are those worthless writings to which Gandhi refers in this angry retort to Indian terrorism? Who were Dhingra's instigators? Obviously the reference is to Savarkar, who was then in London, and his books on *Mazzini* and *The Indian War of Independence of 1857*, as well as his numerous revolutionary pamphlets.

As for Gandhi's charge that Dhingra recited his defence by rote, this may be partly true and partly false. Savarkar did put a written statement into his hands, but this appears to have been confiscated by the police. Soon after, however, the *Daily News* of London got hold of a copy and published it. The report said that 'Dhingra gloried in his own martyrdom'.

The statement itself is a piece of uninspiring writing. It read: 'I admit I attempted to shed English blood as a humble revenge for the inhuman hangings and deportations of patriotic Indian youths. I believe that a nation held in bondage with the help of foreign bayonets is in a perpetual state of war. Since open battle is rendered impossible to a disarmed race, I attacked by surprise. Since guns are denied to me, I drew forth my pistol and fired. The war of independence will continue between India and England so long as the English and Hindu races last.'

Gandhi's disillusionment with the role of the deputation was mounting day by day. Hardly a fortnight after arrival, he reports he is working in conditions which 'can give no pleasure to a satyagrahi'. He is disgusted with meetings with 'so-called big men or even men who are really great. All such efforts are no better than pounding chaff. Everyone appears preoccupied with his own affairs. Those who occupy positions of power show little inclination to do justice. Their only concern is to hold on to their positions.

'We have to spend a whole day in arranging for an interview with one or two persons. Write a letter to the person concerned, wait for his reply, acknowledge it,

and then go to his place. One may be living in the
north of London and another in the south. Even after
all this fuss, one cannot be very hopeful about the outcome.'

All the same, never before was the public relations
man in Gandhi more active than during these hectic
weeks in London. Spurred on, perhaps, by Polak's
unexpected success in India in building up public
opinion for the South African struggle, his determination
to achieve comparable results in London got the better
of him. 'The public meeting in Bombay,' he wrote
to Ampthill, 'was a very great success. Since then
meetings have been held at Surat, Ahmedabad and
Kathore. The Indian press has been discussing the
question at much greater length than heretofore and
certainly much more intelligently. It now recognizes,
as it did not do before, that the Transvaal Indians are
suffering not for achieving a selfish purpose, but for
removing national dishonour.

'I feel that Mr. Habib and I should not go away
without undertaking some public activity. At first
thought, this is what appears to be necessary. We
should address a meeting of such members of the House
of Commons as would care to listen to us; invite assis-
tance and cooperation from all parties; place the position before representatives of religious denominations;
circulate the short statement which has been approved
by you; interview willing editors; and address a general
letter to the press.'

Evidently, Gandhi had already begun to sense that the
main purpose for which the deputation came to London
was going awry. The government was unmoving and
Smuts and company seemed to be having things their

own way. In his letter to the press, referred to above, he put the position succinctly and in perspective. ' If we were fighting not for a principle but for loaves and fishes,' the letter said, ' Mr. Smuts would be prepared to throw them at us in the shape of residential permits etc. But when we insist on the removal of the racial tint implied in his legislation, he is not prepared to yield an inch. He would give us the husk without the kernel. He declines to remove the badge of inferiority, but is willing to change the present rough-looking symbol for a nicely polished one!

' British Indians, however, decline to be deluded. They may yield everything, occupy any position, but the badge must be removed first. The only possible justification for holding together the different communities of the empire under the same sovereignty is the fact of elementary equality. And it is because the Transvaal legislation cuts at the very root of this principle that British Indians have offered a stubborn resistance.'

Further evidence of Gandhi's general feeling of tiredness and frustration over his London visit was that he had begun to toy with the idea of paying a short visit to India before returning to South Africa. He broached the subject first with Ampthill, after two months had gone by without any tangible results. ' Mr. Habib and I are seriously considering whether it would not be advisable for us to go to India, after finishing the work here, and ask for a greater manifestation of public sympathy.' He touched upon the matter a month later, again with Ampthill.

The idea recurs in his letter to Polak written about this time. ' The greatest question,' Gandhi says in that letter, ' is the proposed Indian visit. In reality I should not go to India at all. My place is in the Transvaal. But the reasoning that enabled me to come to London is the reasoning that is applicable to the visit to India.'

Two days later he discussed the matter in his usual dispatch to *Indian Opinion*. ' My own view is that it is in the Transvaal that our main work lies—and even there in its jails. There is but one consideration against this. Our coming here this time was an admission of weakness. We came in the hope that an early solution could be found. The very reason which brought us here will justify our going to India. But, of course, a visit to India will delay our return to South Africa.'

Clearly Gandhi's mind was terribly divided on this rather trite question. Such indecision is untypical of him. Why then was he see-sawing between going and not going? To go or not to go—that is the question! What an un-Hamlet-like Hamlet!

Here he is at it again with Ampthill, quoting from his letter to Kallenbach: ' The Indian tour means two months: one month for the voyage and one month in India. It may even mean more. As a passive resister, I feel that the Indian tour—as indeed this tour—is useless. But thinking from the standpoint of non-passive resisters, just as a few months have been given to London, two more may be added to finish off India.' But Kallenbach had promptly cabled him to ' Return Africa if work finished London.' And to complicate matters, Polak had cabled: 'Very strongly advise you to come.' What was he to do? Summing up his predicament, he tells Ampthill: ' Whether the Johannesburg committee has taken a purely passive resistance view, or whether it is owing to want of funds, it seems that we should abandon the Indian visit.'

He puts a final end to the question by saying no to Polak's cable. 'I feel that I have overstayed my time here. You should therefore do the best you can in India yourself.'

I have dwelt on this at some length because, as it seems to me, the unusual tug in Gandhi's mind, the vacillation, the desire, the involved arguments—all go to show that he did very much want to go to India. Perhaps, deep within him, he had begun to sense— especially after the frustrations of London—that his work in South Africa was drawing to a close and that he must now go to India.

This undercurrent was never wholly absent from Gandhi's thoughts although it surfaced but rarely. For example, more than a year earlier, when a reporter of *The Natal Mercury* asked him: ' Do you think the trouble here produces any effect in India ? ' he answered without a moment's hesitation: ' I certainly think it does.'

His fight in South Africa, he would repeatedly make clear, was not a purely local fight. ' It was not intended to defend merely the rights of the Transvaal Indians but also India's honour.' He went further. ' It is in South Africa,' he once claimed, ' that the Indian nation is being formed. A nation can come into being only when people make sacrifices for the sake of freedom.' Remember he made this bold claim in a widely attended meeting in London, present at which, among others, was Bipin Chandra Pal.

At another such meeting, however, Pal and Gandhi disagreed:

Gandhi: Soul force is far superior to brute force. It is invincible.

Pal: But soul force must be backed by physical force.

Gandhi: In that case, it will not deserve the name of soul force!

This, of course, is that old and perennial argument on which no one really agreed with Gandhi, although many pretended to. Here Gandhi is the loner that he has always been. Here he is the prophet that others will try, but fail, to understand.

Remember Gandhi's third and last incarceration in the year of the traumata? When he was released and the people received him with joy, it was on this return to the motherland that he harped. But his notes were of a higher octave. He spoke of the Hindus and Muslims as the two eyes of India. ' If both the eyes remain unharmed,' he told his eager audience, ' you will prosper. If 13,000 Indians continue to fight in the name of God and if the two communities remain united, you will also be the masters of India. What is happening here will have its repercussions out there.'

Although by the compulsion of circumstances—some would say, by the ways of providence—Gandhi spent the best years of his life far away in a foreign and alien land, it was on India that his eyes were permanently riveted. Not because he was born an Indian, but—paradoxical as this may seem—because his primary identification was with the whole human family. And he believed, within reason or simply as an article of faith, that it was through India that one could best serve the human family.

Talking of the aim of his paper, *Indian Opinion*, he put the point rather finely: ' Our object is to serve the entire human race. But Indians must, of course, first serve India. Instead of doing that, if anyone were to claim that he was dedicated to the service of mankind as a whole, it would be nothing more than a pretence. It would be no service at all.' On the surface the statement is self-contradictory. To understand its inner coherence, one must understand the kind of man that Gandhi was. It is precisely in that direction that this book is moving. To understand Gandhi, the normal yardsticks are worse than useless. It is because most writers on him have used these yardsticks that he seems such a bundle of contradictions, inconsistencies and paradoxes. He is nothing of the kind. He is a complete whole, though like all things human he has his fair share of kinks. We have encountered a good many of them already. The patient reader will encounter many more as he reads on. But let him not be put off by them.

An interesting sidelight is thrown on Gandhi's enigmatic personality by how Doke and Polak assessed his role. When Doke wrote that fine little book on Gandhi—the first and still, in many ways, the finest— he wanted to name it ' Pathfinder ', or alternatively ' Jungle-breaker '. It was at Polak's instance that he named it ' An Indian Patriot in South Africa '. Was Gandhi a patriot or a pathfinder? To me, he is a Promethean and, in any case, not a patriot—oh no! To cut such a giant to the size of a puny patriot—and patriots are a dime a dozen—is to do him a grave injury. If Gandhi was simply a patriot, he was nothing worth! Gandhi himself sheds some light on this, in a letter to Maganlal many years later, when the latter roundly accuses him of having too many irons in the fire. ' You may be sure,' defends Gandhi, ' I don't go seeking work. Which activity, do you think, did I go out of my way to take upon myself? If I had not joined the Khilafat movement, I think I would have lost everything. In joining it I have followed what I especially regard as my dharma. Through this movement I am trying to show the real nature of nonviolence. I am uniting Hindus and Muslims. I cannot leave any field in which I have cultivated some strength. My moksha lies through them. It was for this reason that Doke described me as a pathfinder.'

In other words, even though Gandhi's main focus was on India—and he did very much want to go back to his native land—his work encompassed an ever-widening canvas. Perhaps despite himself, his mental focus was constantly being interfered with.

However, to come back to our story, Polak had made such a success of his public relations mission to India, that there really was no need, at that particular juncture, for Gandhi to have made a month's tour of India. What, after all, could he have achieved in a month? Although a hero in South Africa, and to some extent also in London, there were very few leaders in India who thought much of this obscure barrister and his obscure methods of fighting the British empire. The sole exception was Gokhale.

In his very first letter to Polak, within days of his arrival in London and after being comfortably installed at the luxurious Westminster Palace Hotel in Victoria Street, within hailing distance from the houses of parliament, he wrote: ' You should confine your attention for the time being to those whose names I have specially given you: that is, the Editor of *The Times of India* [perhaps he meant Pherozeshah Mehta who was then acting editor of the paper], Professor Gokhale, and Mr. Behramji Malbari.'

Within days, he also wrote to Gokhale: ' I am most anxious that our leaders should realize the national importance of the struggle. Mr. Polak has been sent as a missionary to do this work. I have asked him to place himself unreservedly under your instructions.

' Our work here is very difficult. We are endeavouring, by private negotiations, to arrive at a settlement. But I know Mr. Smuts too well to put much faith in these negotiations.

' We will continue to suffer in the Transvaal until justice is granted. But we have a right to expect much more than we have yet received from the motherland.'

Polak wrote to Gandhi after his meeting with Gokhale: ' He is not hopeful, but is putting the whole of his energies and organization at my disposal. Agrees to necessity of meeting. Promises to work on Sir P. M. who is holding back. Maps out itinerary. Will arrange everything for the future. Wonderful man. Has most accurate knowledge of facts and principles.

' Huge admirer of yours! Is worn out with overwork, worry and malarial fever. '

Just before leaving London—his mission having totally failed—Gandhi wrote again to Gokhale: ' Polak tells me that overwork and anxiety have ruined your health and that your plain-spokenness has endangered your life. I venture to suggest that you should come to the Transvaal and join us. Our struggle is national in every sense of the term.

' If you came, publicly declaring that it was your

intention to share our sorrows, you would give the movement a worldwide significance, the struggle will soon end and your countrymen will know you better. The last consideration may not weigh with you, but it does with me—for the sake of themselves.

'If you are arrested and imprisoned, I should be delighted. I may be wrong, but I do feel that it is a step worth taking for the sake of India.'

What cheek! Did Gandhi really believe that it was as simple as that to draw a liberal statesman into his revolutionary turmoil? It was, of course, the disturbing news contained in Polak's letter that made him hazard the chance. Polak had written: 'You will see what poor Gokhale has to suffer. He tells me that the Governor sent for him and warned him that his person was in danger. The Servants of India watch him day and night and never let him go out unguarded.'

The direction of Gandhi's thinking is now clear. He no longer wants the Transvaal struggle to be his private baby. He wants it to be an integral part of India's struggle for freedom. He wants the Indian National Congress officially to take cognizance of his lone fight. So did he write to Gokhale: 'I should be pardoned for suggesting that the Transvaal question should have a prominent place on the Congress platform, and nothing can be so effective as for you to say that you would join the struggle.'

So did he also accede to Natesan's request for a message to the Congress, though he thought it was 'rather an awkward thing' for him to do. The message reads: 'At the moment I am unable to think of anything

7

but the task immediately before me, namely the struggle that is going on in the Transvaal. I hope our country-men throughout India realize that it is national in its aim, in that it has been undertaken to save India's honour.

' I may be wrong, but I have not hesitated publicly to remark that it is the greatest struggle of modern times. The sons of Hindustan who are in the Transvaal are showing that they are capable of fighting for an ideal pure and simple. The methods adopted are also equally pure and equally simple. Violence in any shape or form is entirely eschewed.

' Incidentally, the Hindu-Mahomedan problem has been solved in South Africa. We realize that the one cannot do without the other. Mahomedans, Parsis and Hindus—or taking them provincially—Bengalees, Madrasees, Punjabis, Afghanistanees and Bombayites have fought shoulder to shoulder.

' I venture to suggest that a struggle such as this is worthy of occupying the best, if not indeed the exclusive, attention of the Congress. If it be not impertinent, I would like to distinguish between this and the other items on the program of the Congress. The opposition to the laws or the policy with which the other items deal does not involve any material suffering. The Congress activity consists in a mental attitude without correspond-ing action.

' In the Transvaal case, the law and the policy it enunciates being wrong, we disregard it and therefore consciously and deliberately suffer material and physical injury. Action follows and corresponds to our mental attitude.

' If the view here submitted be correct, it will be

allowed that, in asking for the best place in the Congress program for the Transvaal question, I have not been unreasonable.

' Passive resistance is an infallible panacea for the many ills we suffer in India. It is worthy of careful study. It is the only weapon that is suited to the genius of our people and our land.

' India is the nursery of the most ancient religions and has very little to learn from modern civilization— a civilization based on violence of the blackest type, largely a negation of the divine in man, and which is rushing headlong to its own ruin.'

There, in that last paragraph, we see the central gandhian theme—and, indeed, the theme of this book— asserting itself. The paragraph compacts and telescopes, in one savage testament, not only the train of Gandhi's thinking for some fifteen years—from that Christmas dinner speech aboard S.S. *Courland* moored off Cape Town harbour—but its final fruitioning in London, where he had his first brush with terrorist Indian thought and numerous occasions to test his basic thesis with trends in other minds of substance, as well as judge audience reaction whenever he was invited to speak to varied groups.

We must therefore leave our brief sentimental journey to India, in Gandhi's company, and return to London. It is the night of September 7, 1909. After a day of endless work and endless frustrations, Gandhi snatched a brief hour, before retiring, to read Edward Carpenter's *Civilization: Its Cause and Cure*. He was so thrilled with what he read—one is always thrilled when others are seen to be thinking along more or less the same lines as oneself!—that he lost no time in writing about it to Polak. ' A very illuminating work,' he described it.

' His analysis of the civilization that we know is very good. His condemnation, though very severe, is in my opinion entirely deserved. The cure suggested by him is good, but I note that he is afraid of his own logic, naturally because he is not certain of his ground. No man, in my opinion, will be able to give an accurate forecast of the future and describe a proper cure unless he has seen the heart of India. Now you know in what direction my thoughts are driving me.'

Then he has a dig at Polak. ' I do not think I need —and yet perhaps I may—tone down your raptures over what you have seen in the India of Bombay. I know you know that you are seeing westernized India and not the real India. I hope you may be able to see the latter whilst you are there, though I question whether you will.'

It was about this time that the ' discovery ' of the North Pole was creating a wordy sensation around the world. For the first decade of the twentieth century, when modern technology as we know it now was in its infancy, the Peary-Cook achievement was certainly something to be proud about; just as in our time we have rapturized over the space-age firsts of Gagarin and Armstrong. But Gandhi was not only not impressed by the feat, he was thoroughly amused. ' Men have almost lost their heads,' he reports, over the argument as to which of the two first put his foot on the North Pole. ' Newspapers are full of the controversy. Reports about it and reports of football and cricket fill all the space in them.

' It is beyond my understanding what good the discovery of the North Pole has done the world. But such
things are regarded as important signposts of contemporary civilization. What exactly is their importance,
they alone can say who claim to understand these
matters. I for one regard all these things as symptoms of mental derangement.'

The Illustrated London News of September 18 carried
an article by G. K. Chesterton on the awakening in India.
Gandhi read it avidly and described it as ' reasonable
and worth studying'. ' When young Indians talk of
independence for India,' wrote Chesterton, ' I get a
feeling that they do not understand what they are talking
about. I admit these young idealists are fine fellows.
But when I get to know their views, I get bored and feel
dubious about them. What they want is not very
Indian and not very national.

' They talk about Herbert Spencer's philosophy.
What is the good of the Indian national spirit if they
cannot protect themselves from Herbert Spencer?
I am not fond of Buddhism, but its philosophy is not
so shallow as Spencer's. It has some noble ideals, unlike
the latter.

' One of the papers of these young idealists is called
The Indian Sociologist. Do the Indian youths want to
pollute their ancient villages and poison their kindly
homes by introducing Spencer's philosophy into them?

' There is a great difference between a people asking
for its own ancient life and a people asking for things
that have been wholly invented by someone else.
Suppose an Indian said: " I wish India had always
been free from white men and all their works. Everything has its own faults and we prefer our own.

' "There would have been dynastic wars, but I prefer dying in battle to dying in hospital. There would have been despotism, but I prefer one king whom I hardly even see to a hundred kings regulating my diet and my children.

' "There would have been pestilence, but I would sooner die of the plague than live like a dead man. There would have been religious differences dangerous to public peace, but I think religion more important than peace."

' Suppose an Indian said that, I should call him an Indian nationalist. He would be an authentic Indian, and I think it would be very hard to answer him.

' But the Indian nationalists go on saying: " Give me the ballot box. Give us power. Give me the judge's wig. I have a natural right to be Prime Minister. I have a right to introduce a Budget." Now this is not so difficult to answer.

' If voting is such a very important thing (which I am inclined rather to doubt myself), then certainly we the Englishmen have some of the authority that belongs to founders! When Indians take a haughty tone in demanding a vote, I imagine to myself the situation reversed. It seems to me very much as if I were to go into Tibet and demand of the Lama that I should be treated as a Mahatma!

' In writing this I am not opposing Indian nationalism. I am only letting my mind play round the subject. This is desirable when there is a conflict between two complete civilizations.

' Indians, I admit, have a right to be and to live as Indians. But Herbert Spencer is not Indian. His philosophy is not Indian philosophy. All this clatter about the science of education and other things is not Indian.'

What kindred souls—Chesterton and Gandhi! One wonders whether Gandhi made an effort to meet Chesterton. Perhaps not. But he spent a long time reflecting deeply on the brutal truths expressed in the article—with the felicity characteristic of GKC—and wrote to his people in South Africa: ' Indians must reflect over these views and consider what they should rightly demand. What is the way to make the Indian people happy? May it not be that we are seeking to advance our own interests in the name of the Indian people? May it not be that we have been endeavouring to destroy what the Indian people have carefully nurtured through thousands of years? ' There is no doubt that Chesterton's plainspeaking gave Gandhi a salutary jolt at a time when he was struggling with his own ideas and trying to mould them into a coherent pattern.

Gandhi's great moment came when the Hampstead Peace and Arbitration Society invited him to address a meeting at the Friends' Meeting House. This was about a month after the Chesterton article had shaken him up. One can imagine the state of his mind during this period. The main purpose of his having come to London was slowly, but surely, dragging itself to a dead end. He had harboured hopes of a breakthrough for weeks, but now he had no doubt in his mind that he was simply chasing a mirage.

I like to fancy that this was particularly the time when he took his mind away from the parochial interests arising from the fact of his being a member of the Transvaal Indian deputation and allowed it to play round the question of the human family and its future. His mind, evidently, was under great stress. For on the day prior to the Hampstead meeting, he wrote a letter to his son Manilal—but he dated it as from Johannesburg (whereas he was still in London)!

The subject of his speech at Hampstead was 'East and West'. It was clearly a well prepared one and he was setting great store by its effect on his audience. 'The question of East and West,' he began, 'presents a vast and complicated problem. I have had eighteen years' experience of contact between East and West and have endeavoured to study the problem in all its aspects. I feel I may give an audience such as this the results of my observations.

'As I think of the subject, my heart sinks within me. I am afraid I shall have to say many things which may seem repugnant to you. I may have to use harsh words. I may also have to speak against a system under which I have been brought up. I hope you will bear with me if I hurt your feelings.'

The prologue is ominous. The audience fidgets in its seat.

'I shall have to break many idols,' he goes on, 'which I and my countrymen have worshipped. Perhaps many of you in the audience may have worshipped them too. Kipling had said, in his poem, that 'East is East and West is West / And never the twain shall meet.' I consider Kipling's doctrine a doctrine of despair. It is inconsistent with the evolution of humanity. I feel it is utterly impossible for me to accept such a doctrine.

' Another English poet, Tennyson, in his poem called " Vision " has clearly foretold the union between East and West. It is because I believe in Tennyson's vision that I have cast in my lot with the people of South Africa, the Indians there, who are living in very great difficulties. It is because I think it possible for the two peoples of South Africa—the whites and the Indians —to live together in perfect equality that I find myself in that country. If I had believed in Kipling's doctrine, I would never have lived there.

' There have been individual instances of English and Indian people living together under the same rule without a jarring note. What is true of individuals can be made true of nations.

' To a certain extent it is true that there is no meeting place between civilizations. If the barriers between the Japanese and the Europeans are daily vanishing, it is because the Japanese are assimilating western civilization.

' It seems to me that the chief characteristic of modern civilization is that it worships the body more than the spirit. It gives everything for the glorification of the body.

' Take, for example, railways, telegraphs and telephones. Do these tend to help you forward to a moral elevation? When I cast my eyes upon India, what do I find represented there today under British rule? It is modern civilization that is ruling India. And what has it done? I hope I will not shock my hearers when I say that this civilization has done no good to India.

' All that it has done is to give India a network of railways, telegraphs and telephones. And big cities, like Calcutta, Bombay, Madras and Lahore. All these are symbols of slavery rather than of freedom. The modern travelling facilities have, in fact, reduced our holy places, like Benares, to unholy places. I can picture to myself the Benares of old, before this mad rush of civilization. And I have seen with my own eyes the Benares of today. It is now an unholy city.

'I see the same thing here in England that I have seen in India. The mad activity of modern civilization has unhinged us all. Although I am myself living under that very system, I think it is desirable that I should speak to you in this strain.

'I know it is impossible for our two peoples to live together in India until the British government changed its ways. It has offended the religious susceptibilities of the Hindus by sport in their sacred places.

'Unless the present mad rush is halted in India, a calamity must come. One way would be for the Indian people to adopt modern civilization. But far be it for me to say that they should ever do so. India will then be the football of the world and our two nations will be flying at each other.

'India is not yet lost, but she is certainly immersed in lethargy. There are many things about her which cannot yet be understood. But we must be patient. However, one thing is certain. So long as this mad rush lasts, with its glorification of the body, the imperishable soul within will continue to languish.'

Obviously, this could not have been all that Gandhi said in his first major speech in London. But we must assume that it is a fair summary. In any case—within the limited ambit of this book—the summary seems to me to confirm the general trend of his thinking which we have already noticed more than once in the course of our story. For all one knows, the *India* reporter at Hampstead may have left out many of Gandhi's deeper insights into the malaise of modern man, whose significance or relevance he may have failed to understand. Nevertheless, the Hampstead speech marks a major watershed in the development of Gandhi's chiliastic vision and it is certainly a pity that we do not have a verbatim record.

How important the speech was to Gandhi himself is clear from the fact that the very next day he wrote a long letter to Polak, in which, besides describing the meeting, he articulates a 16-point thesis—or, more precisely, testament—setting forth, if nothing else, at least the direction in which his mind is moving. To me the whole thing appears an admirable summary of *Hind Swaraj*—a book yet to be born.

' As you will be seeing practically the whole of India —a privilege I have myself not yet been able to enjoy,' Gandhi writes, rather ruefully as it appears to me, ' I think I should jot down the definite conclusions to which I have almost arrived after more matured observations made here.

' The thing was brewing in my mind, but there was no certain clear light. The heart and brain became more active after I accepted the invitation of the Peace and Arbitration Society to speak to them on ' East and West'. It came off last night. I think this meeting was a splendid success; they were earnest folk, but some insolent questions were put on the South African situation. You will be surprised to learn that even in Hampstead there were enough men to stand up for the tragedy in South Africa and to talk all the claptrap about the Indian trader being a canker and what not.

A dear old lady got up and said that I had uttered disloyal sentiments. In all the questions that were addressed to me, my main purpose was forgotten [usual in most such meetings, but nevertheless a pity].

' The following are the conclusions: *1*. There is no impassable barrier between East and West. *2*. There is no such thing as western or European civilization, but there is a *modern* civilization which is purely material. *3*. Europeans who are not touched by modern civilization are far better able to mix with the Indians than the offspring of that civilization. *4*. It is not the British people who are ruling India, but it is modern civilization—through its railways, telegraphs, telephones and other such inventions. *5*. Bombay, Calcutta and the other chief cities of India are the real plague spots. *6*. If British rule were replaced tomorrow by Indian rule based on modern methods, India would be no better. Indians would then become only a second or fifth edition of Europe and America!

' *7*. East and West can only and really meet when the West has thrown overboard modern civilization almost in its entirety. They can also seemingly meet when the East has also adopted modern civilization. But that meeting would be an armed truce.

' *8*. It is simply impertinence for any man, or any body of men, to contemplate reform of the whole world. To attempt to do so by means of highly artificial and speedy locomotion is to attempt the impossible.

' *9*. Increase of material comforts, it may be generally laid down, does not in any way whatsoever conduce to moral growth.

' *10*. Medical science is the concentrated essence of black magic. Quackery is infinitely preferable to what passes for high medical skill. *11*. Hospitals are the instruments of the devil. They perpetuate vice, misery and degradation, and real slavery. *12*. If there were no hospitals for venereal diseases, or even for consumptives, we should have less consumption and sexual vice among us.

' *13*. India's salvation consists in unlearning what she has learnt during the past fifty years. The railways, telegraphs, hospitals, lawyers, doctors and such like have all to go. The so-called upper classes will have to learn to live the simple peasant life, knowing it to be a life giving true happiness.

' *14*. Indians should wear no machine-made clothing, whether it comes out of European or Indian mills. *15*. England can help India to do this and then she will have justified her hold of India.

' *16*. There was true wisdom in the sages of old having so regulated society as to limit the material condition of the people. Therein lies salvation.'

How any reader will respond to these ' conclusions ' of Gandhi will depend largely on how he is conditioned. Gandhi is a highly prescriptive pedagogue. At the same time he is also highly innovative. To understand his seeming quaintness, one needs to decondition onself. Remember that Gandhi, like any one of us, was a creature of circumstance and the product of a particular age. The medical science, for example, that he is attacking so viciously was a product of Victorian ignorance, cocksureness and plagiarism. One notices here a bit of Chesterton's sarcasm. But it is much more than that. It is a piece of typical gandhian insight. To assimilate what Gandhi is saying, one needs to strengthen one's powers of digestion. He is tough

119

meat—and if he is not to everyone's taste, we can only blame ourselves.

After listing the ' conclusions ' Gandhi goes on: ' There is much more I can write upon today, but the above is enough food for reflection. You will check me when you find me wrong. I have given you a terrible dose. I hope you will be able to digest it.

' You will notice too, that it is the true spirit of passive resistance that has brought me to these almost definite conclusions. I am unconcerned whether such a gigantic reformation, shall I call it, can be brought about among people who derive satisfaction from the present mad rush. The theory is there: our practice will have to approach it as much as possible.

' Living in the midst of the rush, we may not be able to shake ourselves free from all taint. Every time I get into a railway car, use a motor-bus, I know that I am doing violence to my sense of what is right. The visiting of England is bad—and so on. I do not fear the logical result. The chief thing is to put our theory right.

' In India you will be seeing all sorts and conditions of men. Therefore did I feel that I should no longer withhold from you what I call the " progressive step " I have taken mentally. If you agree with me, it will be your duty to tell the revolutionaries that the freedom they want, or think they want, is not to be obtained by killing people but by setting themselves right, and by becoming and remaining truly Indian.

' The future of India lies not with the British but with the Indians themselves. If they have sufficient self-abnegation, they can make themselves free this very moment. When there was no rapid locomotion, traders and preachers went on foot, from one end of the country to the other, not for pleasure or health but for the sake of humanity. Then were Benares and other places of pilgrimage holy cities, whereas today they are an abomination.'

There were at least five other occasions, excluding the farewell meeting, when Gandhi had a chance to speak in London, before large and small audiences, but at none of these did he care to dwell on the ' Hampstead theme '—that is to say, the crisis of modern civilization—although there can be no doubt that this was what was uppermost in his mind. He chose to turn these occasions into business meetings and to speak more or less on the South African Indian problem and related issues of Indian nationalism. After all, he was in London not to sell his private panacea but to seek an honourable settlement of the Transvaal issue or, failing which, at least to gain public and private support for the cause and, as Polak was successfully doing in India, get through a public-relations chore or two in its behalf. Even at the farewell meeting, which was held at the Westminster Palace Hotel and was attended by a large number of luminaries, including Motilal Nehru, he breathed not a word about the Weltansicht which (as he confessed to Polak) had taken violent possession of him. Did he perhaps touch upon the theme when he went out of London to Cambridge to address students at the Indian Majlis (there were some seventy of them, one of whom must have been the young Jawaharlal Nehru) ? Very likely not. Another canvassing job for the Transvaal cause, no doubt.

This is passing strange. Why was Gandhi reticent? Why was he unwilling to open out his heart? Was he disappointed with the non-response to his core ideas at Hampstead and, in particular, with what lay behind it: namely, a conditioned non-perception and the congenital incapacity of the human mind to absorb innovative ideas quickly? Or had he merely begun to feel unsure of himself and decided not to make a fool of himself in public?

And yet, he did enter into an intimate dialogue over this—or tried to do so—with Ampthill. ' I have made it a point,' wrote Gandhi, ' to see Indians here of every shade of opinion. I have endeavoured specially to come into contact with the party of violence. This I have done in order to convince them of the error of their ways.

' Some members of this party are earnest spirits. They wield an undoubted influence on the young Indians here. One of them came to me with a view to convince me that I was wrong in my methods.

' An awakening of the national consciousness is unmistakable. Everywhere I have noticed impatience of British rule. In some cases the hatred of the whole race is virulent.

' Those who are against violence are so only for the time being. They do not disapprove of it. But they are too cowardly or too selfish to avow their opinions publicly.

' I believe that repression will be unavailing. At the same time, I feel that the British rulers will not give liberally and in time. The fault is not of men but of the system; and the system is represented by the present civilization, which has produced its blasting effect as well on the people here as on India.

'The true remedy lies, in my humble opinion, in England discarding modern civilization. This civilization is ensouled by a spirit of selfishness and materialism, is vain and purposeless, and is a negation of Christianity.

'But this is a large order! It may then be just possible that the British rulers do not impose upon Indians this modern civilization. Railways and machinery, and the corresponding increase of indulgent habits, are the true badges of slavery of the Indian people, as they are of Europeans.

'I no longer believe in Lord Macaulay as a benefactor. I do think that a great deal too much is being made of *pax Britannica*. To me the rise of cities like Calcutta and Bombay is a matter for sorrow rather than congratulation. India has lost in having broken up a part of her village system.

'Holding these views, I share the national spirit; but I totally dissent from the methods, whether of the extremists or of the moderates. For either party relies ultimately on violence. And violent methods must mean acceptance of modern civilization, leading to ruinous competition and destruction of morality.'

Although treading some common ground, it will be apparent that Gandhi's letter to Ampthill is different from his letter to Polak in many ways. First of all, the motivation. To Polak Gandhi was selling an idea and asking him, in turn, to sell it for him in India. To Ampthill, Gandhi was presenting himself as a possible candidate for a leadership role in India. Look at these two supplementary statements: (a) 'I should be uninterested in the fact as to who rules. I should expect rulers to rule according to my wish.' (b) 'Whenever I can get the time, I would like to take my humble share in national regeneration and to secure your Lordship's cooperation in that larger work if it ever comes to me.'

Secondly, the emphasis. In the letter to Polak, the emphasis is almost entirely on the crisis of modern civilization and on how 'a gigantic reformation' could be brought about in the world, perhaps through the instrumentality of India. Whereas in his letter to Ampthill, Gandhi not only dismisses the idea as a 'large order' but immediately switches on to issues which are patently political.

Thirdly, the fact that whereas Gandhi's letter to Polak carried the usual gandhian stamp of openness, his letter to Ampthill was tainted with a certain secretiveness wholly uncharacteristic of him. He wrote: 'The information I have given your Lordship is quite confidential and not to be made use of prejudicially to my countrymen. I feel that no useful purpose will be served unless the truth is known and proclaimed.' What truth? And proclaimed by whom?

The mystery is further deepened when we see him sending a copy of the letter to Polak and describing it as 'quite confidential'. 'But of course you should know the whole position. After reading the letter I would like you to destroy it. I am sending a copy to Dr. Pranjivan Mehta [one of Gandhi's long-time benefactors] with a similar request.' What is all this hush-hush about?

Ampthill's reply, as one would expect, is diplomatic, courteous but non-committal. ' I am not yet prepared,' he writes, 'to make any comment on your views, but I fully appreciate their spirit and candour. I must, however, confess that I do not fully understand your arguments and that I am in doubt as to the conclusions at which you have arrived.'

In his letter, Gandhi had hinted that 'if a discussion is considered necessary, I am at your service'. To this Ampthill responded favourably, but the discussion could not take place on account of illness in the latter's family.

Weighing all the factors that surround Gandhi's relations with Ampthill—including the fact that but for the latter, Gandhi's protracted negotiations with the government in London could hardly have even got off the ground—I am inclined to brush aside the uncharitable construction that some have put on this seemingly ungandhian letter. All I would say is that there was a tug-of-war going on in his mind—with India pulling him towards her on one side and the impending crisis of modern civilization beckoning him on the other—and that, as a practical idealist (or, let us say, as simply an astute politician) he found the pull from his native land more difficult to resist, besides being immediately practicable. On the other hand, there is not the slightest doubt that the concern nearest his heart was not India's freedom from British rule—or any rule for that matter—but the liberation of man from the horrors of a mechanistic, sensate, acquisitive and non-humanistic civilization. His predicament thus was one of choice. To which of the two pulls shall he yield first?

This is a core question in the understanding of Gandhi. The seemingly inscrutable Ampthill letter provides one answer. The other and more conclusive answer was revealed to Gandhi after he had left London and was on the high seas. To this final revelation we shall now turn.

The time is November 1909. Gandhi is in the beginning of his fortieth year. Immediately behind him are four weary months of the London smog—both literally and metaphorically. As the steamship *Kildonan Castle* sails out to sea and the English coastline fades out of view, there is a crispness in the air, a freshness, an exhilaration. Perhaps, after all, the time had not been entirely wasted (Gandhi must have thought as he stood on the deck) for had he not had a chance to test the validity, or rather the general acceptability, of his ideas in discussions with a wide spectrum of people, Indians as well as Europeans, young as well as old. There was that brush with Pal. And his talk with the Indian students of Cambridge—bright young fellows—from among whom undoubtedly would come at least some of the dynamic leadership his country so much needed. Well, of course, he could have put to them some of his basic ideas and watched their reaction, but after that Hampstead experience he had decided that he had better leave well alone. All those nights of preparation for the Hampstead speech had gone to waste. There hadn't been a single soul in that large audience who showed any signs of having understood him.

But when he came to think of it all, the pervasive non-perception with which his ideas were greeted did seem to make sense. For what had been his mission to London? He hadn't gone there as a prophet to warn the Europeans of the impending collapse of their civilization. He had gone there simply as part of a two-member deputation to plead the Transvaal Indian case. And the notoriety that preceded him was not that he was some kind of a prophet, with a new burning message for man, but that he was an unusually courageous passive-resister who rather enjoyed going to jail and a somewhat slithery political negotiator to boot. This was his public image. How could he have possibly lived it down in a mere four months? Who had even an inkling of the storms that were raging within him? Not even perhaps his closest associates. All that they knew about him was that he had an infinite capacity of suffering and that out of it he had fashioned a magic wand—satyagraha—with which he fought racist regimes in South Africa and hoped by and by to fight the mighty British empire itself.

And here he was, returning empty-handed to his people, after having spent a precious five hundred pounds sterling from the community's sparse kitty. What lay before him and his people? Freedom, equity, justice, self-respect? Fiddlesticks! The moment he landed he would be arrested and cast into jail—there to keep company with his son, Harilal, and many of the other jail-hardened veterans. Yes, he saw no other prospect. To him it was almost a way of life. He enjoyed the meditative silence of jails much more than the dawn-to-midnight stream of visitors—and the endless drafting of memoranda and dictating of letters—that was his un-happy lot within the luxurious suite at the Westminster Palace Hotel. But what about the others? Was jail-going a way of life for them as well, or were they simply moths buzzing around the incandescence of an idea—his idea—for lack of an alternative of their own?

And so, as night fell, he scampered back into his first-class saloon, his mind in a daze, but hopeful that the next morning would bring him light. At any rate he had heaps of letters to write, since there would be little chance for that once he was back in his convict's clothes. Fortunately there was a liberal supply of the ship's stationery in his drawers and he could always ask for more if he needed them. And apart from the letters, he had his most important chore to perform— producing copy for his magazine.

Morning. Dear old England miles behind him. No land in sight. Nothing but the surging sea all around him. Cut off from the outside world and immersed in his own thoughts, little did Gandhi know that on the very day he set sail, far away in India, at Ahmedabad, terrorist nationalists had tried to assassinate the viceroy, Lord Minto. Violence was dogging his steps wherever he went. It was an aide-de-camp, when he was reaching London four months ago. Now as he was leaving London, it was the viceroy himself! Which was going to prevail in the end—the suffering and self-sacrifice of Gandhi or the bullets and bombs of the terrorists?

The avatar of self-discipline, with the sun full risen, lost little time in chalking out his daily program of work. He would write and write and write. The letters, of course—to his alter ago Maganlal, to his sons Manilal and Ramdas (Harilal being already in jail), to West, perhaps to Gokhale and Polak. And the dispatches to *Indian Opinion*, more pedagogic and instructional than informative. Oh, what a producer of excellent journalistic copy Gandhi always was! A super-journalist, besides being a super-satyagrahi.

But where was he to begin his daily chores? Ah, of course with Tolstoy. His people must know more about this great man. Come to think of it, his most memorable achievement in London was the intimate contact he developed with Tolstoy. Everything else paled into insignificance before it.

Gandhi had written his first letter to Tolstoy on the eve of his forticth birthday. In it he had first given the old sage a brief idea of what was going on in the Transvaal. Then he said, somewhat apologetically: 'Together with a friend, I have come here [that is to say, to London] to see the imperial authorities and to place before them the position, with a view to seeking redress. Passive resisters have recognized that they should have nothing to do with pleading with the government, but the deputation has come at the instance of the weaker members of the community, and it therefore represents their weakness rather than their strength.'

Fine. But Gandhi had two specific thoughts in mind when he wrote to Tolstoy. One of these concerned an essay competition which he wanted to organize as part of his public relations work in London. It was to be somewhat on the same lines as the competition he had held in Johannesburg months ago and which, frankly speaking, produced poor results. The subject was to be 'The Ethics and Efficacy of Passive Resistance'.

'A friend has raised the question of morality,' said Gandhi, 'in connection with the proposed competition. He thinks that such an invitation would be inconsistent with the true spirtit of passive resistance and that it would amount to buying opinion. May I ask you to favour me with your opinion on the subject of morality?' Tolstoy promptly put his mind at rest by saying: 'A competition, that is, an offer of a monetary inducement in connection with a religious matter would, I think, be out of place.'

The other matter on which Gandhi wished to consult Tolstoy concerned the latter's 'Letter to a Hindu', which he had written for an underground journal published from Vancouver, called *Free Hindustan*. 'A copy of your letter,' wrote Gandhi, 'has been placed in my hands by a friend. On the face of it, it appears to represent your views. It is our intention to have 20,000 copies printed and distributed and to have it translated also. We have, however, not been able to secure the original, and we do not feel justified in printing it unless we are sure of the accuracy of the copy and that it is your letter.

'I would also venture to make a suggestion. In the concluding paragraph you seem to dissuade the reader from a belief in reincarnation, which is cherished by millions in India. With many it is a matter of experience, no longer a matter of academic acceptance. It explains reasonably the many mysteries of life. My object in writing this is to ask you if you will please remove the word reincarnation from the other things you have dissuaded your reader from.'

Assuring Gandhi of the genuineness of the letter, Tolstoy wrote: 'As to the word reincarnation, I should not myself like to omit it. In my opinion, belief in reincarnation can never be as firm as belief in the soul's immortality and in God's justice and love. You may however do as you like.'

Although Tolstoy was thus very much in Gandhi's mind, it would be purely conjectural to assume that it was with the translation of his letter that he began his daily chores on the steamer. I like to fancy that

it was to the writing of *Hind Swaraj* that he set himself
from the word Go and that he devoted the best part
of his time to it. Everything else, including the Tolstoy
translation, was sandwiched in between, whenever he
felt weary or desired a diversion. How else can one
explain that in under ten days (he set sail on November
13 and signed his Preface on November 22) he managed
to complete a book of 30,000 words, besides all his other
work? Averaging more than 3000 words of original
writing a day does not come easy even to a professional
writer. And Gandhi, although he did turn out
enormous quantities of writing (most of it journalistic)
during his public career of fifty-years—witness the
elephantine dimensions of his *Collected Works*, already
sixty volumes high, with half as many to come—was
more of a publicist, politician, pedagogue and prophet
than a writer in the strict sense.

That he did slave-drive himself during much of the
voyage is clear from what he wrote to Maganlal.
'There is no end to the work I have put in on the steamer
this time. You will see this from my letters to West
and others, and other writings.'

Or this letter to his second son, Manilal: 'It is
9.30 p.m. now. As I am tired of writing with the right
hand, I write this to you with the left. I may have to
go to jail straight on landing; that's why I am writing
whatever I can now. I take it that you at any rate
will rejoice at my going to jail, for you have understanding.'

To Ramdas, his third son: 'I write this to you as I
do not know when we shall meet. Don't be angry
with me if I haven't brought anything for you. There
was nothing I liked. What could I do if nothing

European appealed to me? I like everything Indian. The people of Europe are good, but not their way of life. Don't be upset if I go to jail. Rather you should rejoice. I should be where Harilal is.'

But before we begin our detailed look at *Hind Swaraj*, which is where this book will logically end, let us briefly glance at the other things he wrote. Take his two prefaces to the Tolstoy letter, one in Gujarati, the other in English. The reader should remember that the letter was not published in *Free Hindustan* to which it was originally sent, since the terrorist editor of that paper could not bring himself to agree with Tolstoy's views.

Writes Gandhi: 'To me Tolstoy's letter is of great value. Anyone who has enjoyed the experience of the Transvaal struggle will perceive its value readily enough. But those who have not known what a happy experience satyagraha can be, who have been caught up in the toils of this huge sham of modern civilization, like moths flitting round a flame, will find no interest in Tolstoy's letter all at once. Such men should pause for a moment and reflect.

'No one should assume that I accept all the ideas of Tolstoy. I look upon him as one of my teachers. The central principle of his teaching, as set out in the letter, is entirely acceptable to me.

'It is a mere statement of fact that every Indian has national aspirations. But there are as many opinions as there are Indian nationalists, on the exact meaning of that aspiration and more especially on the methods to be used to attain the end.

'One of the methods to attain the end is that of violence. Tolstoy's life has been devoted to replacing the method of violence for removing tyranny or securing reform with the method of non-resistance to evil. He would meet hatred expressed in violence with love expressed in self-suffering.

'India, the nursery of the great faiths of the world, will cease to be nationalist, whatever else it may become, when it goes through the process of civilization, when gun factories and other manifestations of hateful industrialism come up on its sacred soil.

'If we do not want the English in India, we must pay the price. Tolstoy indicates it. " Do not resist evil," he says, " but do not also yourselves participate in evil —in the violent deeds of administration of law courts, collection of taxes, and what's more, of the army. Then no one in the world will enslave you."

'Who can question the truth of what he says in the following? "A commercial company," he says, with derision and in sorrow, " enslaved a nation comprising 200 millions. Tell this to a man free from superstition and he will fail to grasp what these words mean. What does it mean when 30,000 people, not athletes but rather weak and ill-looking, have enslaved 200 millions of vigorous, clever, strong, freedom-loving people? Don't the figures make it clear that not the English but the Indians have enslaved themselves? "

'There is nothing new in what Tolstoy preaches. But his presentation is refreshingly forceful and his logic is unassailable.'

It will be more in keeping with the style of this book if we look at the chiliastic phase of Gandhi's life by beginning, so to speak, at the wrong end: that is to say, by examining the reactions of others to his Weltansicht, as haltingly portrayed in *Hind Swaraj*. Logically, then, we should start off with his rank antagonists.

I cast about for a name. In the early part of his political career in India Gandhi had more antagonists than admirers. He was looked upon as an upstart (despite his phenomenal record in South Africa), a crank, an ignoramus and a relative mediocrity. But not all the antagonism arose from knowledge of what it was that the upstart was trying to say and do. The antagonists—well, practically all of them—took him for other than what he was. They tried to shove him into the wrong pigeonhole and when he didn't fit they took umbrage on him. It is amazing that none of these so-called wise men of India ever thought of trying to find for Gandhi another pigeonhole or at least to enlarge what they had, so that it may fit a giant!

But one of the antagonists—less a national leader and more a defender of the raj—did come close to identifying the core of the upstart's message. This was Sir Sankaran Nair. In the early nineteen-twenties he had the courage of his convictions to publish a scathing attack on Gandhi. The book was called *Gandhi and Anarchy*. It was an honest book and a painstaking one.

Here is a rather random sampling of Sankaran Nair's assessment of Gandhi. 'There is scarcely any item in the Gandhi program,' writes the intrepid author, 'which is not a complete violation of everything preached by the foremost sons of India till 1919.' The perception is faultless. With one stroke of the pen he demolishes the myth that Gandhi represented a logical continuation of the Indian renascence which began in the late nineteenth century. The myth is not dead. It is being perpetuated in the endless stream of historico-political studies on Gandhi that continue to fill the bookshelves.

'Some politicians, the author continues, 'who naturally desire to use him, and the influence he has acquired for putting pressure on the government to concede further reform, also have joined him. There are of course many genuine patriots who, believing in the efficacy of his methods to obtain Home Rule, also follow him. But I am satisfied he is using them all to further his own ends—an attempt in which he is bound to fail.' That last sentence is a classic piece of insight, except for the parenthesis. For Gandhi did succeed in using all the stalwarts of his time to further his own ends—or at least in browbeating them into silent, if sullen, acceptance. Lest the reader should misunderstand me, I ought to explain that whereas Sankaran Nair was using the phrase 'to further his own ends' in its usual pejorative sense, I am giving it a larger meaning. To fight for an idea which is burnt deep into your soul is to further your own end. Without this ingrained procrusteanism in our great men, civilization would have ossified at a primitive level long ago. Gandhi came to India with a cast-iron blueprint in his pocket and he was hell-bent on its universal acceptance.

With an accumulating insight, the author goes on to point out that 'in order to understand the nature of the agitation now carried on by Mr. Gandhi in India, it is necessary to understand his mentality and his real views on various questions that are now in debate. These are given in his book, *Indian Home Rule*.' It is amazing how unerringly he points to the core of the man, when greater men than him hardly even noticed its existence.

Sankaran Nair then proceeds to analyze the book in

some detail. Here of course he trips and falls. I do not blame him. *Hind Swaraj* injected into the mental climate of that time such a whole congeries of shocks that few could have survived its impact without tripping and falling. However, some of his observations are worth quoting, if only to bring out their negative force.

Here is a telescoping of a few of his more significant observations. 'Gandhi's tirade against machinery and mill industries, on account of the evils he has witnessed in the West, is due to his ignorance. A little knowledge, in his case, has proved a dangerous thing!

'There is no harm, perhaps, as long as such fantastic visionaries restrict the application of these principles to themselves, to their own persons or properties. But it becomes a serious matter when their general application is sought for.

'Mr. Gandhi, to take him at his best, is indifferent to facts. Facts must submit to the dictates of his theories. The only difficulty in his way is that they don't!

'Will o' the wisp politics are of no use to a people who have to live in a world which, from long and bitter experience, has at last come to realize that dreams of distorted brains are not the stuff of which contented nations are made. Gandhi, in fact, is seeking not only to destroy the fruits of the long endeavour of the constitutional reformers, but to blast for ever any hopes of Indian regeneration.'

Well, well! But let's hear Sankaran Nair to the very end.

'I believe,' he concludes, 'that Mr. Gandhi is honest in his self-hypnotization. I believe he does not really know what he is doing. At least that is the only possible charitable assumption when we watch his feats of political acrobatics which have the power of deluding such vast numbers of people, making them passionately intolerant, violently intolerant often, of the slightest criticism of their hero.'

When I first read *Gandhi and Anarchy* many years ago, I realized the truth of an old saying: that in order to understand a man in a true historical perspective, one must go to those of his contemporaries who opposed him rather than to those who supported, admired or followed him. For in all hero worship—even if the hero is not one with feet of clay—there is that unavoidable element of fawning which numbs your critical imagination and exposes you to sycophantic delusions. True, the opponent suffers a like distortion. But the blurs are easily detected and you can sweep them aside and get at the truth.

Three legendary examples come to mind. Ravana understood Rama with a finesse that is to be seen in none of the other characters of the *Ramayana*. Similar was the unspoken rapport that existed between Kamsa and Krishna in the *Bhagavata*. But most to the point is the story told about Vasishta and Visvamitra, two renowned sages of Hindu lore who were in deadly opposition to each other. In the course of one of their encounters, Vasishta's wife Arundhati noticed that her husband was engrossed over the writings of his opponent. On her expressing surprise, Vasishta said: 'Why not, my dear? I must go into the views of my opponent thoroughly before I can hope to counter them.' A piece of apocrypha, doubtless. But it makes an important point.

Of course, Sankaran Nair is but one among several

heavy-weight opponents of the Gandhi line. But the others, for a reason I cannot fathom, never came within hearing distance of *Hind Swaraj*. If they did, they simply brushed it aside as a piece of juvenilia. This is passing strange. For when I first heard about *Hind Swaraj*—long before I got down to reading it—I knew instinctively that if one seriously desired to understand Gandhi, it had to be through that book and through nothing else.

So much for the kind of criticism that Gandhi's contemporaries could muster against him. What about his modern critics? They are objects of ridicule, if not pity. Here is a brief sampling from Dhananjaya Keer's recent (heavily prejudiced) biography of the man.

Keer wears his ignorance and lack of perception without a visible touch of remorse. In the original edition of *Hind Swaraj*, says Keer, 'Gandhi condemned parliamentary democracy. But in the Preface of 1921, he said that he was working for parliamentary swaraj, in accordance with the wishes of the people of India. It was a paradox that he should help to introduce a system that he himself considered ruinous. And yet he asserted that he withdrew nothing from his original booklet!'

Small minds have always found it difficult to enter into the soul of a great idea. A giant like Tolstoy, on the other hand, at the merest glance understood the meaning of *Hind Swaraj* in its full sweep. The evidence is there in his diary, on two successive days in April 1910. The first entry: 'This morning two Japanese arrived. Wild men in ecstasy over European civilization. On the other hand, the book and the letter of the Hindu [meaning Gandhi] reveal an understanding of all the shortcomings of European civilization and even of its total inadequacy.' Second entry: 'Yesterday I read Gandhi on civilization. Wonderful!'

Keer, the Savarkar zealot that he is, is not content with misconstruing Gandhi. He must smear Tolstoy as well. Look at this fantastic piece of speculation: Tolstoy, he says, 'must have discarded Gandhi's views on western civilization and encouraged him to write against the Indian extremists and revolutionaries in India!'

Three cheers! Gandhi needed no goading to fulminate against violence, whether in India or elsewhere. That was his stock-in-trade. But let's leave the blind men behind and look at those who had eyes to see. They did not all see equally well. But each one of them had a glimmer of what it was that Tolstoy's Hindu was trying to communicate. And a glimmer is a great deal.

Some three decades after the book came to be written and published—and for some time proscribed by the Raj as a tract conducive of sedition—the Indian theosophists suddenly saw light. Perhaps they saw in *Hind Swaraj* a reaffirmation of the Blavatskian gospel, as enunciated in such works as *Isis Unveiled*.

Talking of the world's debt to India, Madame Blavatsky had said in her time: 'No people in the world have ever attained to such a grandeur of thought, in ideal conceptions of the deity and its offspring man, as the Sanskrit metaphysicians and theologians. It is to India that all the other great nations of the world are indebted for their languages, arts, legislature and civilization.'

Gandhi never laid it on as thick as all that. When

9   **139**

he pitted the wisdom of ancient India against the unwisdom of modern civilization, he did so with much modesty. Look at this message which he sent to the Indian theosophists, at their request, for publication in their journal, *Aryan Path*, which carried a broad-spectrum symposium on *Hind Swaraj*.

'I welcome,' wrote Gandhi, 'your advertising the principles in defence of which *Hind Swaraj* was written. If I had to rewrite the booklet I might change the language here and there. But after the stormy thirty years through which I have since passed, I have seen nothing to make me alter the views expounded in it. The reader should know that it stopped the rot that was about to set in among some Indians in South Africa. Against this he may balance the opinion of a dear friend—who, alas, is no more—that it was the production of a fool!'

The dear friend referred to is undoubtedly Gokhale, who despite his enormous admiration and support for Gandhi, never did get down to understanding the long and lone vision contained in *Hind Swaraj*. Passing strange again!

Commenting on Gandhi's message, the editor of *Aryan Path* wrote: 'For this curse of civilization [which was the burden of Gandhi's epochal book] Madame Blavatsky gave a cure in her writings, which contain principles and applications. But these were not practised on any large scale even among those who called themselves theosophists.

'When Gandhiji wrote his *Hind Swaraj* and advocated, in his own way and words, almost the same cure, there were many—and not only "a dear friend"—who called him: "Thou fool!"

'There are many who think that the disease of this civilization is not curable and that death must result. There are others who, hoping for a radical recovery, suggest a variety of panaceas, most of which are devoid of real guiding principles. "Civilization is not an incurable disease," says Gandhiji.

'Not only is India's own future bound up with her acceptance or rejection of Gandhiji's teachings in building her own civilization founded upon immemorial moral principles, but that of the world also.' The editor, being a theosophist, appears to be pitching it as high as Madame Blavatsky did in the nineteenth century. Gandhi was more down to earth. Even when he spun his utopias, his feet remained firmly planted on the ground.

But let's look at the chief contributors to the *Aryan Path* symposium. Take Frederick Soddy, the British Nobel laureate in chemistry. Soddy, with the adroitness typical of a scientific mind, takes little time in identifying the strength of *Hind Swaraj*. It is, he says, 'the absence of mere word-spinning and sophistry which characterizes the book. It's all as pat as that, take it or leave it, and to this no doubt it owes its power.'

His focus is on the gandhian political doctrine of nonviolence. 'The interest in this remarkable doctrine,' he says, 'lies of course in its immediate measure of political success, and anyone who wishes to change the world would do well to study it.' But he is candid and he has an amiable dig at Gandhi's attack on the machine civilization. 'Having only just returned from a visit to India [the year, the reader will remember, is 1938] the writer can honestly say he saw little outwardly there to suggest it, except perhaps a certain race consciousness. On the other hand, the internal combustion engine seems to have been at least as busy there as elsewhere in altering the mode of livelihood of peoples —not to attempt any more profound analysis of the situation.'

J. D. Beresford, the novelist and pacifist, goes a little deeper. While admitting that Gandhi would not turn the Englishmen out of India 'even if the thing could be done peacefully,' he is certain in his mind that 'Gandhi's gaze is steadily fixed on an ideal that can never be realized under English rule'. Indeed, he argues, 'as a matter of practical service to the present condition of India, Gandhi's gospel will be of no more value than was the same gospel preached by Gautama to India twenty-four centuries ago.'

Novelist Claude Houghton quotes Lord Lothian's opinion that '*Hind Swaraj* contains in embryo everything that Gandhi is now teaching'. Then, with a Kiplingesque twist, he asserts: 'That a man with the beliefs of Gandhi is a mighty force in India, shows that India and England are not different countries—they are different worlds.' However, he concedes that 'it does seem probable—the state of Europe being what it is [Hitler was already on the rampage]—that this doctrine of passive resistance will not be dismissed contemptuously as the dream of a super-crank'.

There is a fine touch of perception in biographer Hugh Fausset's analysis. 'This is a profoundly revolutionary little book,' he says, without the slightest hedging, 'and the fact that it is addressed to Indians and is concerned with their specific problems does not make it less relevant to Englishmen, though it may be harder for them to accept it. For the whole purpose of the book is to save India, not from Englishmen, but from the modern civilization which is eating into the vitals of the West.'

In *Hind Swaraj* Gandhi had said: 'Machinery is the chief symbol of modern civilization. It represents a great sin.' No equivocation. Straight from the shoulder. Fausset takes this masterly insight a step farther. 'Machinery,' he says, 'is in fact the outward embodiment of the split in man's being, which at present it deepens, tending everywhere to deaden his creative spirit.'

But, he admits, 'to speculate on the future of the machine is a waste of time. We should concentrate all our energy upon the restoration of man to his true estate. And it is because Mr. Gandhi has devoted himself to this task with unflagging sincerity that *Hind Swaraj*, containing as it does the core of his teaching, is one of the best modern handbooks of that real revolution which must happen in us all, if we are to fulfil the creative purpose of life.'

Another important contribution to the symposium came from essayist Gerald Heard. Writing rapturously, but not without an eye on logic and reason, he says: '*Hind Swaraj* is one of those books about which it may be said that they are not so much books as great natural phenomena. Rousseau's *Social Contract* was such a book. Another was Marx's *Das Kapital*. Such books, important as they are in what they say, are infinitely more important in what they do.

'Yet *Hind Swaraj* is superior to the other two. It is more significant because it does not mark, as did each of those, the end of an age but the beginning of a new order. They were symptomatic of western man

143

awakening to a new sense of self-consciousness, feeling himself to be "born free but everywhere in chains". Using the same technique which had mastered him— namely, violence—these newly aware individuals would break their chains and chain their masters! Therefore these revolutions led inevitably to reaction, leaving new tyrants more firmly on the thrones.

'Realizing this fact, Gandhi opened a new path. He put into practice a new means—the right means— which alone can lead to the right end. For, as the Buddha taught, only correct means will lead to desired ends. Wrong and evil methods can only lead to wrong and evil results.'

A piece of juvenilia, they had called it—Gandhi's renowned colleagues and mentors in India. Not only Gokhale. Jawaharlal had once written, no doubt in utter despair over the master's seeming lack of logic and reason: 'Bapu, you are infinitely greater than your little books!'

Against this, let us look at what novelist Irene Rathbone said in the same symposium. 'The language of the book,' she asserted, ' is simple and logical; the form of its dialogue: it is economical, condensed, poetic. And enormously powerful.' I leave it to the reader to decide which opinion to choose.

Rathbone goes on: 'But perhaps I could not have paid that book a greater compliment than to have found myself forced by its tremendous honesty to search my own honesty. I would implore people to read it. It is not dated—not in any essential way. It is suffused in light. It gleams with cogent passages: phrases at which the mind wistfully, assentingly smiles.'

John Middleton Murry's assessment and critique of *Hind Swaraj* is perhaps the profoundest thing yet written on that book and it deserves to be examined at some greater length. He ends by calling *Hind Swaraj* 'the greatest book that has been written in modern times'. This of course is an asseveration and like all asseverations must be taken as nothing more than a half-truth. The value of the critique lies mainly in the deep-searching questions that it raises.

For example, take the deep inner contradiction in Gandhi's rejection of parliamentary democracy in *Hind Swaraj* and his subsequent espousal of 'parliamentary swaraj' as a legitimate goal for the Indian freedom movement. Hostile critics like Dhananjaya Keer see in such contradictions, not struggles of the soul, but dishonest antics. God help them!

Now look at how Murry dwells upon the contradiction. 'In spite of its clarity and beauty,' he muses, '*Hind Swaraj* confronts us with the awkward question: how far, in allying himself with the nationalist political movement in India, Gandhi had negated his own religious philosophy. "If India copies England," he had concluded, with reference to establishing parliamentary government, "it is my firm conviction that she will be ruined." One cannot refrain from asking how Gandhi justified to his own mind his devotion of his "corporate activity to the attainment of parliamentary swaraj". The contradiction appears to be insuperable and it is hardly to be wondered at that Gandhi refers to "writings which suggest that I am playing a deep game and using the present turmoil to foist my fads on India."

'True, no reader, sensitive to the moral beauty of the vision of *Hind Swaraj*, could possibly suppose that Gandhi was playing a deep game; but the contradiction is only the more bewildering. Perhaps he decided that it was worth any sacrifice to establish the idea and practice of nonviolence in the Indian nationalist movement. I conjecture that the crucial decision, for Gandhi, must have lain here; and that he convinced himself that the establishment of nonviolence as a mere technique of political pressure, even though in pursuit of ends diametrically opposed to his own, would in fact ultimately promote his real ends and not the ostensible ones. This is not, indeed, to play a deep game, but it is something which cruder souls would thus describe.'

Be that as it may. Gandhi's 'practical idealism' (which sounds to me no different from Karl Popper's idea of 'piecemeal social engineering') makes short shrift of the contradiction; and let us waste no more time over it. The values of Murry's critique lies elsewhere.

Says he: 'What Gandhi means by real swaraj, as distinct from and even diametrically opposed to parliamentary swaraj, would be expressed in Christian idiom as something between the establishment of the Kingdom of Heaven on earth and the restoration of the primitive village-community. By calling it something between the religious dream and the historical fact, I do not at all imply that it is a hybrid.

'I find it impossible to discern any essential difference between Gandhi's vision of real swaraj and what I believe to be the authentic Christian vision of the Kingdom of Heaven. But there are distinctions. One is that Gandhi can make his vision concrete by turning to the actual village-community which still survives in

India; whereas the Christian thinker has to turn to the village-community of the European Middle Ages.

'Another is that whereas Gandhi has made up his mind that the technical civilization of Europe is altogether evil and is to be wholly rejected, the European Christian thinker is compelled to ask himself whether it is not absolutely necessary to preserve some basic elements of the mechanical technique: first, because European life is now so completely bound up with them that it would collapse into ruin if they were withdrawn; and secondly, because the same spiritual imagination which can conceive as a reality a society based on Love (which is Gandhi's swaraj) can also conceive that such a society could just as well make true and humane use of the machine. For although the machine has so disastrously become the master instead of the slave of European civilization, it does nevertheless offer an immense and universal liberation from human drudgery. Simply to reject it, as Gandhi does, is to declare that mankind is inherently incapable of using the most tremendous and, therefore, the most ambiguous gift of God except to its own damnation.

'Probably it is the fact that at the present stage of human evolution, mankind is incapable of using the machine except to its own perdition. And it seems quite doubtful whether mankind can pass beyond its present stage except at the price of universal disaster—which takes all meaning from that "beyond". But are we not, as spiritual beings, compelled to believe that the advance is possible? To put it otherwise, does not Gandhi's own belief in "the gospel of love" compel him also to believe that love can control even the machine to the purposes of love?

147

'I do not see how Gandhi can escape this conclusion except by dogmatically holding the position that the spiritual life, or the life of love, can be lived only in primitive communities, which are artificially made inaccessible to the temptation of the machine.

'Gandhi, if I understand him aright, would object to the word " artificially " here and would say that there was nothing artificial in the conscious decision of a community to reject the machine. And that is true, up to a point.

'But does not the very achievement of the spiritual insight sufficient to resist the introduction of the machine, necessarily also imply the achievement of the self-discipline to use the machine beneficently? In other words, if satyagraha is a real condition permeating and inspiring a community, must not that community obviously possess the wisdom and self-control to use the machine for truly communal ends?'

How flawlessly persuasive Murry sounds! And yet, we must remember he was writing in 1938—aeons away from the present reality of a runaway technology. Had he been writing today, after the four terrible decades of terror and trauma through which it is a miracle we have survived, would he have argued with the same confidence? I doubt it. But let us hear him to the end.

'To declare,' says Murry, 'as Gandhi does in *Hind Swaraj*, that the machine is just simply evil, and necessarily and for ever creative of evil, seems to me finally to be turning one's back on the actual perplexity of mankind.

'Gandhi's apparent conception that any mechanical aid to the capacities of the unaided man is unnatural and evil is surely arbitrary. "I should like to add," he says, "that man is so made by nature as to require him to restrict his movements as far as his hands and feet will take him."

'I am very far indeed from regarding such a statement as absurd. On the contrary, I think Gandhi is trying to bring into currency an all-important but forgotten truth. But I also think he makes the mistake of trying to state it so simply that it becomes false. The very spinning-wheel he loves is also a machine. On his principles it should be abolished!'

Tut tut! Murry, in making that naive rebuttal, seems strangely unaware that he is committing the very fallacy of which he is accusing Gandhi—the falsification that results from simplicism. But let that pass.

'The profound truth,' he goes on, 'of which Gandhi is one of the greatest prophets, is that nature—considered as a pattern of the harmonious life of man—is indeed our guide. But he forgets that nature grows and expands, and that the true guidance of nature is discovered only in man—and, alas, through human suffering. Thus, and not otherwise, is the discovery made that if man does not submit his new powers to the rule of love, he must end by destroying himself.

'The guidance of nature is not given, as a simple datum, to man; it is revealed to him by suffering. We cannot look back on any actual order of society and say, "There nature reigned, there love was supreme". It was not.

'The pre-machine community may be a more human and spiritual society than the mass-society produced by the machine. But its weakness is that it has no power of resistance against the machine. In so far as

Gandhi believes that it has, he appears to me mistaken.

'I agree with him that the only power which can resist the devastation of the machine is the soul-force of love. But precisely that power was not in the pre-machine community; if it were, the machine would have done no harm!'

That fallacy of simplicism again!

The soul-force of love, Murry goes on, ' is not in any natural community, because it is developed only in the twice-born soul. That power, of definite and conscious self-renunciation, may just as well be used to control the machine than to annihilate it.

'Thus I am forced to the conclusion that the social goal of the spiritual leader in the modern world should be not to withdraw to the pre-machine community but to advance towards the creation of a society capable of using the machine without incurring material and spiritual self-devastation.'

No, however profound Murry's analysis seems on the surface, he somehow continues to revel in phantasy. Which is a pity. For more than any other thinker of that period—some three decades after *Hind Swaraj* was written—he seems to me to come closest to Gandhi's vision. If he misses it by a whisker, and no more, yet it is too big a miss. Not for nothing did Gandhi bewail and beseech his critics to 'read *Hind Swaraj* with my eyes.'

But then, and finally, Murry makes up for the miss with a full-throated asseveration of the gandhian prophecy: 'Assuredly, I see absolutely no hope for western " civilization " except the kindling of a vast and consuming flame of Christian love. The choice appears to be between that, or mass-murder on a scale at which the imagination sickens.'

150

Well, with Hitler's hordes already goose-stepping athwart the face of the European heartland, any Englishman across the Channel could have said something on those lines. The shape of things to come was already writ large everywhere. What makes Murry's prophecy significant is the way he links it all up with Gandhi.

'If the miracle should come to pass in Europe,' writes Murry, 'it will not be all our doing. The influence of Gandhi will have counted for much. He has reminded us that the way of nonviolence is a possible way out of the horrors into which the mass-democracies of Europe are preparing to plunge.'

Therefore, concludes Murry, 'the greatest Christian teacher in the modern world is Gandhi; and *Hind Swaraj* is the greatest book that has been written in modern times.'

After that *tour de force*, there is very little one need garner by way of appraisals, contemporary or otherwise, of the meaning of *Hind Swaraj*. Indeed, after that perceptive exercise in *Aryan Path*—and for this, much thanks to the Indian theosophists—Gandhi's great little book has virtually remained untouched and dust-laden on the shelf. Let me, with your permission, dear reader, take the book from the shelf, blow off the dust and invite you to accompany me on an exploration. Into what? Why, into the mind, heart and soul of Gandhi—the very core of the man.

That old problem again. Where shall I begin? For while others have been silent or cynical or scornful about *Hind Swaraj*, Gandhi lost no chance to return to its teaching and point out—amidst, I am sure, muffled bursts of derisive laughter—its quintessential quality.

A few quick facts about the 'publishing history' of the book—its genesis having already been glanced at—may be useful, especially to young readers, to help keep things in historical perspective.

Gandhi wrote *Hind Swaraj*, like much else of his seminal work, in his native tongue, Gujarati. It was serialized, in two large instalments, in his South African weekly journal, *Indian Opinion*, which was of course bilingual (namely, English and Gujarati: earlier, the journal also carried sections in Hindi and Tamil) immediately after his return from London. A month thereafter it was published as a booklet and, as one would expect, copies were despatched to India. The Government of Bombay were quick to sense its long-run incendiary character and seized perhaps most of the consignment.

When news of the seizure reached Gandhi, he expressed his anguish in a tone which finely blended pity with anger. Said he: 'But we have no right to complain. The Government of India are in a state of panic. Wishing to do something, they intend to stop the circulation of literature that shows the slightest independence of spirit. This overzeal is bound to kill itself.

'We sympathize with them in their desire to stop the spread of methods of violence. We would do and give much to stop it. But the only way we know to eradicate the disease is to popularize passive resistance of the right stamp. Any other way, especially repression, must inevitably fail in the long run.'

Of course he didn't stop just with writing his piece

in his journal. Not Gandhi! He at once set about publishing the booklet in English. 'It is not a literal translation,' he explained, 'but it is a faithful rendering of the original.

'Whilst opinions were being invited as to the advisability of publishing the work, news was received that the original was seized in India. This information hastened the decision to publish the translation without a moment's delay. My fellow-workers shared my view and by working overtime they have enabled me to place it before the public in an unexpectedly short time.'

Then he made some observations, largely apologetic, about the complexion of the booklet. 'I am quite aware,' he said, 'of the many imperfections of the original. The English rendering, besides sharing these, must naturally exaggerate them, owing to my inability to convey the exact meaning of the original.

'Some friends have objected to the dialogue form. I have no answer to offer except that Gujarati readily lends itself to such treatment and that it is considered the best method of treating difficult subjects. Had I written for English readers in the first instance, the subject would have been handled in a different manner.'

I am not so sure. *Hind Swaraj* is so clearly patterned on Blavatsky's *Key to Theosophy*—a brilliant work on a 'difficult subject' whose influence upon him Gandhi has acknowledged—that he might have saved himself the bother of an apology.

Touching the book's forfeiture in India, he expressed surprise. 'There is in the book,' he complained, 'not a trace of approval of violence in any shape or form. The methods of the British Government are undoubtedly severely condemned. To do otherwise would be for me to be a traitor to truth, to India, and to the Empire to which I own allegiance.

'My notion of loyalty does not involve acceptance of current rule or government, irrespective of its righteousness or otherwise. I am not so much concerned about the stability of the Empire—I must frankly confess—as I am about that of the ancient civilization of India which, in my opinion, represents the best that the world has ever seen.

'My countrymen impute the evils of modern civilization to the English people and believe that it is they who are bad and not the civilization they represent. My countrymen, therefore, believe that they should adopt modern civilization and modern methods of violence to drive out the English.

'*Hind Swaraj* has been written to show that they are following a suicidal policy and that, if they would but revert to their own glorious civilization, either the English would adopt the latter and become Indianized or find their occupation in India gone!'

Once the English version was ready, *Hind Swaraj* attained the wider audience it deserved. The most important person to see it at this early stage was Tolstoy. I have already referred, in passing, to the depth and percipience with which the sage responded to its inner meaning.

In sending the book to Tolstoy, Gandhi wrote: 'I am most anxious not to worry you, but if your health permits and you can find the time to go through it, needless to say I shall value very highly your criticism of the writing.'

In his prompt reply, Tolstoy wrote: 'I read your book with great interest because I think that the question you treat in it is of the greatest importance not only for India but for the whole humanity.

'I am at present not quite well and therefore abstain from writing to you all that I have to say about your book and your work, which I appreciate very much. But I will do it as soon as I feel better.'

The letter was touchingly subscribed 'your friend and brother'. But alas, the sage never lived to keep his promise. That year—1910—two great persons died: Tolstoy and Florence Nightingale.

Next in importance, in Gandhi's own estimation, was Gokhale. To him Gandhi had sent, through Polak, a typed copy of the translation, as it would have been futile to send the printed book. The Government of Bombay, with their vigilant tag on Gandhi and his activities in South Africa, would have quickly confiscated it, as they did with the Gujarati original.

Writing to Gokhale, Gandhi said: 'The views expressed by me in *Hind Swaraj* have not been formed without much thought and consideration. If you have had the time to go through it, I shall esteem your opinion.'

Of course Gokhale read the typescript avidly, but his reactions were the reverse of Tolstoy's. He thought the work was crude and hastily conceived and he hoped that, after spending a year in India, Gandhi would on his own destroy it! What a shockingly bathetic way—pathetic too—of opening oneself to a work of genius.

Well, what is sauce for the goose is not necessarily sauce for the gander. Our judgements vary because

10   **155**

our assumptions vary. It is as simple as that. Even so when great men trip and fall—as, with hindsight, we can now say about Gokhale—our hearts cave in.

Perhaps, for a change, we may turn to the reactions of a relatively unknown person. Same period. The man is W. J. Wybergh, a Transvaal legislator-friend of Gandhi's. Gandhi and Wybergh exchanged two long letters which touched upon the salient features of the book. Wybergh is critical, at times hostile, but always persuasive. Gandhi defends his thesis with rare humility and acumen.

Let me try and summarize the pros and cons in the form of a dialogue.

> *Wybergh:* I don't think that on the whole your argument is coherent or that the various statements and opinions you express have any real dependence upon one another.
>
> *Gandhi:* I am painfully conscious of the imperfections and defects you point out. I know how unworthy I am to handle the very important problems dealt with in the booklet. But having had the position of a publicist forced upon me by circumstances, I felt bound to write. The choice lay between allowing readers of *Indian Opinion* to drift away in the matter of the insane violence now going on in India, and giving them a lead, no matter how humble.
>
> *Wybergh:* On many questions of fact, you are at variance with ordinary opinion. While, as a rule, you avoid giving any occasion for specific charges of disloyalty, yet there are so many subtle hints and ambiguous expressions,

so many things left unsaid, and so many half-truths put forward, that I am not at all surprised at anyone considering the book highly dangerous.

Gandhi: I agree that a superficial reader will consider the pamphlet to be a disloyal production. Also that those who will not distinguish between men and measures, between modern civilization and its exponents, will come to that conclusion.

Wybergh: You discourage violence, but only because you think violence is both wrong and ineffective, not because the object sought is wrong!

Gandhi: You're right—provided that it is ever possible to detach the object from the means adopted to attain it. I doubt it. I think Home Rule obtained by violence would be different in kind from that obtained by the means suggested by me.

Wybergh: Very well. On the far more important general principle underlying your book, I must say definitely that I think you are going wrong. European civilization has many defects and I agree with many of your criticisms. But I don't believe that it is 'the Kingdom of Satan' or that it ought to be abolished. It appears to me a necessary step in the evolution of mankind, especially manifested in and suitable for western nations. While I recognize that the highest ideals of India—and of Europe too—are in advance of this civilization, yet I think also, with all

157

modesty, that the bulk of the Indian population require to be roused by the lash of competition and the other material and sensuous as well as intellectual stimuli which 'civilization' supplies.

Gandhi: I have ventured utterly to condemn modern civilization because I hold that the spirit of it is evil. It is possible to show that some of its incidents are good, but I have examined its tendency in the scale of ethics. History teaches us that men who are in the whirlpool will have to work out their destiny in it; but those who are still outside its influence and have a well-tried civilization to guide them, should be helped to remain where they are, if only as a measure of prudence. I have tested the life which modern civilization has to give, as also that of the ancient civilization, and I cannot help strongly contesting the idea that the Indian population requires to be roused in the manner suggested by you.

Wybergh: You are practically preaching liberation, in the religious and metaphysical sense, as the immediate aim of all humanity. For that is what your Swadeshi, in its best sense, as illustrated throughout the book, really means. Now you may have arrived at the stage where it is right to make this the immediate ideal, but the bulk of humanity have not. And I agree with Mrs Besant when she says that there is a real danger in preaching liberation to people who are not ready for it.

Gandhi: Liberation in the sense in which I

have used the term is undoubtedly the immediate aim of humanity. It does not, however,
follow that the whole of humanity can reach
it in the same time. But if liberation is the
best thing attainable by mankind, then I
submit it is wrong to lower the ideal for anyone.

Wybergh: To turn now to the still more
general application of your ideals: I think you
are confusing between passive resistance and
non-resistance. What you call soul force and
passive resistance have nothing to do with love
or spirituality in themselves. In advocating
these things instead of physical force, you are
only transferring the battle and the violence
from the physical to the mental plane. Your
weapons are mental and psychic, not physical,
but also not spiritual. You are still fighting to
win—and fighting harder than ever. In my
opinion, all fighting in modern times is tending
to become more and more a matter of intellectual and psychic force and less of physical force.
It is not thereby becoming more moral or less
cruel, rather the reverse, but it is becoming
more effective.

Gandhi: I admit that the term 'passive
resistance' is a misnomer. I have used it
because, being a popular term, it easily appeals
to the popular imagination. However, its
underlying principle is totally opposed to that
of violence. It cannot therefore be that the
battle is transferred from the physical to the
mental plane. Violence obtains reform by
external means, passive resistance (soul-force)

by growth from within: that is, by self-suffering and self-purification. The fight of a passive resister is not less spiritual because he fights to win. Indeed he is obliged to fight to win, that is, to obtain mastery of self.

Wybergh: Well, personally, I have grave scruples about employing soul-force for the attainment of physical or political objects, however strongly I may believe in the value of those objects and the justice of my cause. In political life it is often a great temptation to me to do so. But while, of course, I regard all possible means of intellectual persuasion and argument as right and necessary, I think the use of soul-force for concrete ends is dangerous in the extreme. Here I always have in mind the refusal of Christ to use soul-force for even the perfectly harmless and apparently legitimate purpose of making stones into bread. I think that in this story a very profound truth is conveyed.

Gandhi: Your argument tends to show that there must be a complete divorce between politics and religion or spirituality. That is what we see in everyday life under modern conditions. Passive resistance, on the other hand, seeks to rejoin politics and religion and to test every one of our actions in the light of ethical principles. That Jesus refused to use soul-force to turn stones into bread only supports my argument. Modern civilization is at present engaged in attempting just that impossible feat!

Wybergh: Let me make myself clear. It does not follow from what I said that those who, even while using wrong methods, are unselfishly working for a cause (however mistaken) will not reap for themselves the moral and spiritual benefit which follows upon all unselfish sacrifice. I am sure you will do so and are doing so, but I think this is not due to your methods but in spite of them, and that it is actually due to your motives.

Gandhi: No, I can't hold with you that motives alone can always decide the question of a particular act being right or wrong. An ignorant mother may, from the purest motives, administer a dose of opium to her child. Her motives will not cure her of her ignorance nor, in the moral world, purge her of the offence of killing her child. Recognizing this principle and knowing that, in spite of the purity of his motives, his action may be utterly wrong, a passive resister suffers only in his own person.

Wybergh: Taking the passive resistance movement as a whole, on the assumption that what you are really aiming at is not merely a political object but the assertion of the superiority of non-resistance, of love and of true inner freedom, as against the compromises and conventions of life, it does not seem consistent that you should allow yourselves to be regarded as martyrs, or complain of the hardships of prison (not that you yourself have, I believe, ever done this), or make political capital out of what seems to you injustice or ill-treatment, or indeed allow the matter to be advertised in the press or send deputations to England and India and generally carry on a political agitation. If it is really a matter of religion, then I think that the truest heroism consists in suffering as private individuals and saying nothing about it.

Gandhi: I agree with you entirely that a pure passive resister cannot allow himself to be regarded as a martyr, or complain of the hardships of prison, or make political capital out of what may appear to be injustice or ill-treatment. Much less may he allow any matter of passive resistance to be advertised. But all action unfortunately is mixed. Purest passive resistance can exist only in theory. The anomalies you point out only emphasize the fact that we are, after all, very fallible human beings. But I can assure you that, as the struggle progresses, pure spirits are certainly rising in our midst.

Wybergh: Of course, if the object is political, all these things become questions of tactics and may be very proper and useful weapons according to circumstances. Personally, while I admire heroism displayed in a political cause —and the very real heroism of many passive resisters—I must say that it seems in no way superior to the more active forms displayed by soldiers or rioters or revolutionaries. Neither does it differ from them or deserve more sympathy. The physical sufferings of a soldier vastly exceed those of passive resisters; yet, if he should complain that the bullets are too hard, the campaigning is uncomfortable or that the enemy is treating him most unkindly, he would be regarded as simply ridiculous.

Gandhi: I freely admit that all passive resisters are not fired with the spirit of love or of truth. Some of us are undoubtedly not free from vindictiveness and hatred. But the desire in us all is to cure ourselves. Those who became passive resisters simply under the glamour of newness of the movement, or for selfish reasons, have fallen away. Pretended self-suffering cannot last long.

It is necessary to discuss the subject of passive resistance somewhat impersonally. I agree with you entirely that the physical sufferings of soldiers vastly exceed those of passive resisters—of the Transvaal. But the sufferings of world-known passive resisters who deliberately walked into funeral pyres or into boiling cauldrons were incomparably greater than those of any soldier it is possible to name.

Wybergh: Finally, I come to the question of non-resistance itself, and its proper use and place. It appears to me that for the individual saint seeking liberation—for whom the time has come when the personality has to be killed out and the whole world order transcended, in order that the pure spiritual consciousness may unfold—non-resistance may be the right course. But as a practical political principle, suitable for adoption by ordinary men living the ordinary life of citizens, it seems to me altogether pernicious and utterly disastrous to the public welfare. It is mere anarchy, and I have always regarded Tolstoy, its principal apostle, as very likely a saint personally, but when he preaches his doctrines as a political propaganda and recommends them for indiscriminate adoption, as the most dangerous enemy of humanity.

I have no manner of doubt that governments and laws and police and physical force are absolutely essential to average humanity. They are as truly natural, in their stage of development, and as truly moral as eating and drinking and propagating the species. To undermine them without being ready to substitute something else a little better, but still of the same character, is simply to destroy the possibility of all advance.

It is a fatal confusion to suppose that what is right for the saint is right for everyone else. When all humanity has reached sainthood government will become unnecessary—but not till then. Meanwhile civilization must be mended, not ended.

Gandhi: I cannot pretend to speak for Tolstoy. But my reading of his works has never led me to consider that, in spite of his merciless analysis of institutions organized and based upon force—that is, governments —he in any way anticipates or contemplates that the whole world will be able to live in a state of philosophical anarchy. What he has preached—as, in my opinion, have all world-teachers—is that every man has to obey the voice of his own conscience, be his own master and seek the Kingdom of God from within. For him there is no government that can control him without his sanction. Such a man is superior to all government.

And can it be ever dangerous for a lion to tell other lions who, in their ignorance, consider themselves to be lambs, that they too are lions? Should the lion who knows sit still and not ask his fellows to share his majesty and freedom?

Who wins over whom in this frank and forthright exchange of ideas will remain a matter of individual judgement. But never before—and perhaps never after—was the thesis elaborated in *Hind Swaraj* subjected to such percipient grilling. Hence have I dealt with it at such length. At places Wybergh seems more convincing; at others Gandhi. The reason, as I see it, is that the two minds are working at two different levels. Of course Wybergh is visibly biassed in favour of the kind of Home Rule that Annie Besant was propagating. Gandhi borrowed the nomenclature from Annie (hence was the English edition of *Hind Swaraj* called *Indian Home Rule*—as one may reasonably presume) but not her methods. This was entirely typical of Gandhi—a man with his mind fully made up and determined to follow his own lone track, come what may.

There are, I would admit, many ways of watching Gandhi's step as he trailed his lonely pilgrimage over his second, and last, stretch of forty years. Much the commonest of these ways is what may be called the

chrono-historical biography. Books of this kind are
aplenty: they still keep coming. Largely cannibalistic
in style and method, they feed on one another, trying
desperately to reveal some unsuspected sharp turn,
uncover some hidden nuance, pull out another half-
skeleton from the cupboard, or just lift up the carpet
to show what the devout have swept under it. If you
know the trick, this kind of unveiling of Gandhi is easy.
All you have to do is fill the second half of your book
with a junk-heap of documentation—tapes, secret files,
interviews, and you know what. And to hell with the
apocryphal fallibility of human memory.

The psycho-biographical way is another. Not as
common as the first , but increasingly becoming popular
(god help us!). Here the basic assumption is that
almost everything an individual thinks, says or does
springs from one or more psychoneurotic loci. Locate
these and the rest is easy.

These two ways, divergent though they are in many
respects, share a strange fascination for what may be
called the linear supposition. That is to say, that our
mental progression is as much unilinear as our physical
progression—birth, growth, decay, death—is. To anyone familiar with the history of ideas, this supposition
is plainly a fallacy. Human ideas do not necessarily
move in one direction. Nor do they necessarily keep
moving for that matter. Sometimes they are static,
sometimes they retrace their steps, sometimes they
reach a point beyond which they just can't go for
whatever reason.

My way in trying to understand Gandhi has been
largely bio-philosophical. That is why I have called
this little book an experiment in philosophical biography.

But whatever the way—and it is, in the ultimate analysis, not an easy matter to assert that one way is superior to another, only that they are different—we all have to begin with certain postulates. What my postulates are I have frankly set forth earlier. These have led me to the unshakable conviction that Gandhi's mental progression came to a dead stop with his writing of *Hind Swaraj*. Thereafter, he moved not an inch—neither forward, nor backwards, nor sideways. He did not have to. At the time he wrote that book his mind had reached its fullest maturity. He had experienced enough, thought enough, exposed himself enough to the full blast of all that modern civilization had to offer, that the years ahead brought him no fresh revelations; only confirmations of his worst fears.

My book can therefore be brought to a close in one of two useful ways. I can work up a summary of *Hind Swaraj*. This I reject without hesitation. Such a summary is unnecessary and could be misleading. Gandhi's litttle manifesto is such an easy gulp that I will not pamper the reader with easier sips. No, definitely not. If he hasn't the patience to read the whole of *Hind Swaraj*, he had better not read my book either.

The other way is to give the reader a glimpse, just a string of episodes, to show how often, how steadfastly and how relentlessly Gandhi returned again and again to *Hind Swaraj*. Indeed, he performed this act so shamefacedly—after all, how many of us can have the courage or the gumption to return to our own oracles at the merest turn of the screw?—that I sometimes wonder. But no, Gandhi's sticking to his oracle is a thing apart. It is 100 per cent genuine. Therefore it is to giving that glimpse that the last pages of my book will be devoted

On the spinning-wheel: 'I have nothing to withdraw from what I have said about machines in *Hind Swaraj*, and a reference will show that I have included the printing press in the machines. I do not suggest today (1924) a destruction of all the machines, but I am making the spinning-wheel the master-machine'.

'It was in London, in 1909, that I discovered the wheel. It was then that I came in close touch with many earnest Indians—students and others. We had many long conversations about the condition of India and I saw as in a flash that without the spinning-wheel there was no swaraj. I knew at once that everyone had to spin. But I did not then know the distinction bet-ween the loom and the wheel, and in *Hind Swaraj* I used the word loom to mean the wheel!'

'Were we not under the hypnotic and desolating spell of the city civilization, we would realize that only a little combined, conscious and honest effort is required to take the wheel to every cottage in India. Multiply the return of one wheel by, say, one hundred million and the result will convince the most confirmed unbelie-ver of its potency. But probably he will refuse to be willing and say: "What you say is true as an arithmetical problem; it is wholly untrue as a practical proposition." Well, you can only take a willing horse to the trough!'

'As people keep opposing the spinning-wheel, my faith in it gets ever stronger. Don't think I am stupid and stubborn and stick to a thing unintelligently. I placed the spinning-wheel before India only four or five

years ago (c. 1920), but I had put forward my arguments in its favour in *Hind Swaraj* before ever having
set eyes on the spinning wheel.'

'A friend asked me whether I proposed to replace
railways with country carts, and if I did not, how I
expected to replace mills with wheels. I told him that
I did not propose to replace railways with carts, because
I could not do so even if I wished. Three hundred
million carts could not destroy distance. But I could
replace mills with wheels, because here it was a question
of production, in which the wheel could easily compete
if there were enough hands—as there were in India—
to work.'

'I have never tried to make anyone regard the spinning-wheel as *his* kamadhenu or universal provider
but I have certainly regarded it as *my* kamadhenu. Why
should then the intelligentsia feel disgusted if, with
crores of my fellows, I lose my head and make the
spinning wheel my kamadhenu? When in 1909, on
board the *Kildonan Castle*, I declared my faith in
the spinning-wheel in the pages of *Hind Swaraj*,
I stood absolutely alone. Will then my God, who
guided my pen into making that declaration of faith,
abandon me when it is put on its trial?'

I have put before the reader this brief sampling of
Gandhi's thoughts on the spinning-wheel not only
because it is literally the hub of his *Hind Swaraj* thesis
but also to show that, far from being rigid, his thinking
had a fluidity and inner coherence all its own. For a
very specific example of this, contrast these two statements. 'It may be considered a heresy,' he said in
the first edition of the book, 'but I am bound to say
that it were better for us to send money to Manchester

and to use flimsy Manchester cloth than to multiply mills in India.' In the Hindi edition of the book, published eleven years later, he had this to say: 'My views in regard to mills have undergone this much change. In view of the present predicament of India, we should produce in our own country all the cloth that we need, even by supporting, if necessary, mills in India rather than buy cloth made in Manchester.'

On modern civilization: Gandhi's alter ego, Maganlal, was one of the earliest, within his inner circle, to have misgivings about the strange ideas articulated in *Hind Swaraj*. On his unburdening his mind, Gandhi wrote to him: 'There is no doubt that we shall have to go back to the extent to which we have imbibed modern civilization. This part of the task is the most difficult one, but it will have to be done. When we take a wrong path there is no alternative but to retrace our steps.

'We have got to free ourselves from attachment to the things we are enjoying. For this it is necessary that we begin to feel disgust for them. Whatever means and instruments appear to us to be beneficial are not going to be given up. Only he who realizes that there is more harm than the apparent benefit from a particular thing will give it up.

'I personally feel that no benefit has been derived from our being able to send letters quickly. When we give up railways and such other means we shall not bother ourselves about writing letters.'

Then this broadside. 'Please do not,' Gandhi reprimanded Maganlal, 'carry unnecessarily on your head the burden of emancipating India. Emancipate your own self. Even that burden is very great. Apply everything to yourself. Nobility of soul consists in realizing that you are yourself India. In your emancipation is the emancipation of India. All else is make-believe.'

In a similar vein, Gandhi wrote to Maganlal on another occasion: 'It is sad that a great man like Gokhale is engrossed in a thing like the Servants of India Society. I believe he will come out of it, for he is honest. It is simply an indifferent imitation of the West. Is it proper for the "servants" to have servants to cook for them? And what a superstition that only an M.A. or B.A. could become a "servant"!

'What we are doing in Phoenix is the real thing. What goes on in Poona—leaving aside the motive, which is good—is unreal. The condition of my mind at present is that of "neti neti". Even Phoenix is "neti". Yet, comparatively, it is better than the pomp and show of Poona.

'Acording to the standard indicated by me in *Hind Swaraj*, the work of Gokhale's "servants" is likely to add to our slavery. If I tried to turn East into West, I also would sigh like Gokhale and lose heart. My present state of mind is such that even if the whole world were against what I have written, I would not be depressed.

'We do not aspire to improve India; we want to improve ourselves. That alone can be our aspiration, all the rest is false. The servant's knowledge of English has become a camouflage for them. We have to rid ourselves of the fetish of literacy and mundane knowledge.'

Evidently Gandhi was smarting under the ridicule that Gokhale, with a shocking lack of percipience, had

poured upon his prided work. There is no doubt that
Gandhi had taken Gokhale's endorsement of his thesis
for granted. A misfiring of two minds! 'It is not
for me to argue,' he pleaded, when his expectations
went haywire, ' but should I ever have the privilege of
meeting you personally, I shall certainly again press
upon your attention some of the views I hold so strongly,
and which it appears to me are perfectly sound.'

The mood of anger and loneliness continues in a
letter he wrote to Narandas. Said he: 'We should
not think that persons of the stature of Prahlada and
others do not exist in India even today. We shall meet
them when we deserve. They are not to be found in
the chawls of Bombay. You may live in Bombay, as
you like, but be quite sure that Bombay is a veritable
hell, absolutely useless.'

When Gandhi was still in London, there was quite a
stir there as well as in other European capitals over
the execution in Spain of the atheist educator Ferrer.
G. K. Chesterton, in a letter to the *Daily News* of London,
exposed the hollowness of it all. He wrote: 'We
have been hysterically protesting against what Spain
has done, but that is so much hypocrisy and nothing
else. In fact, we are just as bad as Spain, in certain
respects much worse. We have no political executions
in England because we have no political rebellions in
our country and not because we are a religious people.
Wherever we do have rebellions, there we do have
executions, much more mean, reckless and savage than
the execution of Ferrer.'

The alert salesman that he was, Gandhi made capital
out of this to prop up his attack on western civilization.
'We saw in *Hind Swaraj*,' he wrote, 'that it is not so

much from British rule that we have to save ourselves as from western civilization. The writings of Englishmen themselves tell us how wicked western civilization is. In view of the shortcomings of this civilization which dazzles us so much, we had better consider whether we should tolerate it in India or banish it while we have still time to do so. It is a civilization which grinds down the masses and in which a few men capture power in the name of the people and abuse it. The people are deceived because it is under cover of their name that these men act.'

A glimpse of the turmoil in Gandhi's mind is to be had in his letter to West. 'As you know,' he wrote, 'my mind is never at rest. I am now trying bold experiments. The thoughts I have put across in my article on the ethics of hawking [the majority of Indians in South Africa were either hawkers or petty traders] only foreshadows what is coming in my life. The more I observe, the greater is my dissatisfaction with modern life. I see nothing good in it. Men are good, but they are poor victims making themselves miserable under the false belief that they are doing good. I am aware that there is a fallacy underneath this; and I may be a deluded fool. This risk all of us have to take. The fact is that we are all bound to do what we feel is right. And with me I feel that modern life is *not* right. The greater the conviction, the bolder my experiments.'

Often Gandhi's attack on modern civilization was misunderstood as an attack on the West. An example of this can be seen in an address presented to him in Orissa in 1934. Among other things, the address praised him for having shown the incompatibility between East and West! Much amused, Gandhi said that if this were true of him, it would be a matter not of praise but of reproach.

'I am a follower of advaita,' he said. 'East and West, South and North are all one to me. A sworn opponent of untouchability in every shape and form, how dare I make an untouchable of the West! What I have really said is that it will be suicidal for us to imitate modern civilization—miscalled "western" because it comes from the West. Modern civilization stands for indulgence, while ancient civilization attached great importance to self-denial and self-restraint. It is therefore a conflict not of East and West but of two widely divergent philosophies of life.'

In a discussion with students in Calcutta, in the same year, he threw fresh light on his *Hind Swaraj* thesis. 'Let us not,' he said, 'be obsessed with catchwords and seductive slogans imported from the West. Have we not our own distinct eastern traditions? Are we not capable of finding our own solution to the question of capital and labour? What is the system of varnashrama but a means of harmonizing the difference between high and low, as well as between capital and labour?

'All that comes from the West on this subject is tarred with the brush of violence. I object to it because I have seen the wreckage that lies at the end of this road. The more thinking set even in the West today stand aghast at the abyss for which their system is heading.

'I have been a sympathetic student of the western social order and I have discovered that underlying the fever that fills the souls of the West there is a restless search for truth. I value that spirit. Let us study our eastern institutions in that spirit of scientific inquiry and we shall evolve a truer socialism and a truer communism than the world has yet dreamed of. It is surely wrong to presume that western socialism or communism is the last word on the question of mass poverty.

'We cannot afford to blindly imitate the West. In the West, if they do certain things they have antidotes for them too; we have not. Take the instance of birth-control. It may seem to work well there, but if we took to it as it is being advocated in the West, in ten years there will be a race of eunuchs in India!'

An American educationalist, on a visit to India, questioned Gandhi about his 'methods'. 'Not many methods,' chuckled Gandhi, 'but the one method of unadulterated truth and nonviolence.'

'But you might ask me,' continued Gandhi, 'how are truth and nonviolence expressed and applied? I would say at once that the central fact in my program is the spinning-wheel. I know that Americans are startled when I say this. What can be the meaning of this pet obsession, they ask.

'When as a nation we adopt the spinning-wheel, we not only solve the question of unemployment but we declare that we have no intention of exploiting any nation, and we also end the exploitation of the poor by the rich.

'We can never industrialize India unless, of course, we reduce our population from 350 millions to 35 millions, or hit upon markets wider than our own and dependent on us. It is time we realized that where there is unlimited human power, complicated machinery on a large scale has no place.'

The infuriating innocence of the ideas expressed in

11–A

Hind Swaraj earned Gandhi many intellectual tormen-
ters. Here is one of them. He wrote to him: You
say, machinery has been the bane of civilization. Then
why do you allow yourself to travel in railway trains
and motor cars?'

'Well,' said Gandhi, 'there are certain things which
you cannot escape all at once, even whilst you are
avoiding them. This earthy case in which I am locked
up is the bane of my life, but I am obliged to put up
with it and even indulge in it. But does one seriously
doubt that the machine age was responsible for the
organized murders during the late war [the first world
war]? Asphyxiating gas and such other abominations
have not advanced us by an inch.'

Here is another. 'Would you be so intolerant,'
he asked Gandhi, 'as to call the revolutionaries ignorant
because they cannot understand your peculiar dogma
of nonviolence?'

'Not at all,' said Gandhi. 'There is no difference
between the view expressed in *Hind Swaraj* and the
views now expressed by me. The Bengal revolutionaries
undoubtedly shed the fear of Englishmen. That was a
distinct service to the country. But bravery and self-
sacrifice need not kill.

'It should be remembered that *Hind Swaraj* was
written in answer to the revolutionary's arguments and
methods. It was an attempt to offer him something
infinitely superior to what he had, at the same time
retaining the whole of his spirit of self-sacrifice and
bravery. I call him ignorant not merely because he
does not understand or appreciate my method but
because he does not even appear to me to understand
the art of warfare!'

Katherine Mayo, in an interview in 1926, prodded Gandhi on some aspects of his *Hind Swaraj* thesis. One of these concerned man's rabid craze for faster modes of travel—the horse buggy at one end and Concorde at the other. 'All of these,' Gandhi hit back, 'are coming to smother us, not to deliver us. I can only say I hope that we shall be spared that affliction. But it may be we shall have to drink the bitter cup. If we do not learn from the experience of the West, we may have to drink it. But I am leaving no stone unturned to avoid that catastrophe.'

The utopianism inherent in the book was another thing that bothered many of Gandhi's critics. To these his characteristic response was: 'I do not think it is right to say that the principles propounded in *Hind Swaraj* are not workable just because I cannot practise them perfectly.' Or again: 'Even if I am not able fully to implement the ideas expressed in *Hind Swaraj*, I think there is nothing wrong in claiming that those ideas are correct.'

Others took *Hind Swaraj* to be the fruit of a deep-seated anti-western fixation in Gandhi. What a foolish thought! Gandhi was, despite his outward appearance, thoroughly western in his ways of thinking. 'I am no indiscriminate, superstitious worshipper of all that goes under the name of "ancient",' he once hit out. 'I have never hesitated to demolish all that is evil or immoral, no matter how ancient it may be. Nevertheless I must confess I am an adorer of ancient institutions, and it hurts me when, in their rush for everything modern, people despise all their ancient traditions and ignore them in their lives.

'We of the East very often hastily conclude that all

that our ancestors laid down for us was nothing but a bundle of superstitions. But my own experience has led me to the conclusion that, whilst there may be much that is superstitious, there is a lot more that is not only not superstitious but, if we understand it and reduce it to practice, gives life and ennobles one. Let us not therefore be blinded by the hypnotic dazzle of the West.'

The cornerstone of Gandhi's evaluation of anything is whether it is genuine. 'I am a passionate devotee of simplicity in life, but I have also discovered that it is worthless unless the echo of simplicity comes from within. The organized artificiality of modern life cannot have any accord with true simqlicity of heart. Where the two do not correspond, there is always either gross self-deception or hypocrisy.'

Also whether the base is solidly spiritual. 'The West,' he once retorted, to a persistent interlocutor, 'may have physical and mental strength, but where does it have spiritual strength? Since all its strength is related to what is opposite of brahmacharya, it has proved to be fatal to the progress of the world in the right direction. That is why I have called it monstrous. Had western civilization been built on the ideal of brahmacharya, the state of the world today would have been very different. Instead of being pitiable, it would have been attractive.'

But then, as it has often been argued, wasn't the Indian renascence which began with Ram Mohun Roy the result of exposure to western culture? True, said Gandhi. 'Every one of the Indians who has achieved anything worth mentioning in any direction is the fruit, directly or indirectly, of western education. At the same time, whatever reaction for the better he may have had upon the people at large was due to the extent he retained his eastern culture.

'Of myself, whilst I have freely acknowledged my debt to western culture, I can say that whatever service I have been able to render to the nation has been due entirely to the retention by me of eastern culture to the extent it has been possible. I should have been thoroughly useless to the masses as an anglicized, de-nationalized being, knowing little of, caring less for, and perhaps even despising, their ways, habits, thoughts and aspirations.

'All kinds of winds—poisonous winds, in my view—are blowing into the country from the West. There are, of course, some beautiful currents too, like Tolstoy's life. But these do not blow with every ship that arrives! Along with other foreign goods, foreign literature also arrives. Its ideas intoxicate our people and draw them to the path of self-indulgence.

'Do not be vain and believe that your thoughts—or what in your immaturity you have read in books and understood from them—are the only truth, that what is old is barbarous and uncivilized, and that truth lies only in things newly discovered.

'I have nothing to be ashamed of if my views on ahimsa are the result of my western education. I have never tabooed all western ideas, nor am I prepared to anathematize everything that comes from the West as inherently evil. I have learnt much from the West and I should not be surprised to find that I had learnt something about ahimsa too from the West. It is enough for me to know that my views on ahimsa have now become a part and parcel of my being.'

In an interview to the *Chicago Tribune*, in 1931, Gandhi was asked: 'Sir, twenty-three years ago you wrote a book, *Hind Swaraj*, which stunned India and the rest of the world with its terrible onslaught on modern western civilization. Have you changed your mind about any of the things you have said in it?'

'Not a bit,' came Gandhi's reply, trippingly on the tongue. 'My ideas about the evils of western civilization still stand. If I republish the book tomorrow, I would scarcely change a word.'

Elsewhere, Gandhi expressed himself even more forcefully: 'The western civilization which passes for civilization is disgusting to me. I have given a rough picture of it in *Hind Swaraj*. Time has brought no change in it. What the westerners worship under the name of civilization is a golden vessel. Its glitter has begun to dazzle us also.' Oh, the pity of it all!

In the foregoing pages, all that I have tried to do is to give the reader a pointillistic image of the strange mould in which Gandhi's mind was cast. I have done this by putting together a random scatter of the ways in which he met criticisms of *Hind Swaraj*—the book to which he clung like a leech throughout his life. It was not some pathological fixation but a conviction springing from the very depths of his being. It brought him into a headlong clash with practically all around him, and especially Jawaharlal Nehru—but that's a long story and I shall not burden my book by getting entangled in it.

'Read *Hind Swaraj* with my eyes,' Gandhi kept pleading. But alas, none would listen to him, none would care to understand him.

Except perhaps the ordinary men and women of India. To one such group Gandhi once summed up—with an exquisite succintness hard to improve—the meaning of his great little book.   Here is what he said.

'This is not a mere political book.   I have used the language of politics, but what I have really tried to offer is a glimpse of dharma. Hind swaraj means Ramarajya or the rule of dharma.   Just as one cannot help speaking when one's heart is full, so also I have been unable to restrain myself from writing the book because my heart was full.'